Praise for *EdTech Essentials, 2nd Edition*

Monica Burns, EdTech leader extraordinaire, is a teacher's best friend, an administrator's ally, and a student's greatest advocate in the world of EdTech and learning. This book is her greatest yet: a brilliant and thoughtful guide for how to make the EdTech experience matter, deepen our work with students, and invigorate teaching and learning on every level. She is a caring, humanizing voice for excellence in teaching and learning with EdTech warming our journey and giving us and our students tools for success. Don't miss *EdTech Essentials*!

—**Pam Allyn**, literacy expert, author, and activist

Monica Burns has done it again. Filled with practical information, *EdTech Essentials* narrows down the most vital areas for classroom technology use to make sure students are being supported in every way they interact in digital spaces. Whether you are an administrator supporting teachers and making plans for your school year or a teacher looking to infuse high-quality digital learning experiences into your lessons, this book will help you prioritize the skills that matter most and give you the tools you need to guide your students' growth as creators, consumers, and collaborators. Filled with today's most robust tools and resources that you can use tomorrow, *EdTech Essentials* should be the next book on your professional reading list!

—**Thomas C. Murray**, director of innovation, Future Ready Schools, Washington, D.C.

Through her extensive experience and vast knowledge of educational technology, Monica Burns has created a resource that every educator will benefit from. Her book focuses squarely on what the learner can and should be doing with digital tools to develop needed competencies in a rapidly changing world. Although technology continues to change at a rapid pace, Monica reminds us that it is effective pedagogy that matters above all else. This easy read is packed with practical strategies that can be used immediately.

—**Eric Sheninger**, associate partner, International Center for Leadership in Education and bestselling author

D1716396

As a trusted education leader, Monica Burns continually publishes inspiring yet practical guides to help teachers of every level. This fresh update of *EdTech Essentials* adds sections on artificial intelligence, media literacy, and a host of new resources that educators can use to guide their practice. Monica brings clarity to complex topics, providing easy-to-understand definitions, workflows, and ideas for those of us too busy to keep up with the rapid changes in tech. The title is spot-on: whether you're a novice or a technology power user, this is an essential book for every educator, learning coach, and education leader.

—**Michael Hernandez**, award-winning teacher
and author of *Storytelling with Purpose*

In this updated edition of *EdTech Essentials*, Dr. Monica Burns not only revisits the core themes that made the original a must-read but also weaves in fresh perspectives that highlight the emerging role of AI in education. This book is an excellent starting point for those seeking direction while trying to keep up with the rapid pace of today's EdTech world.

—**Dr. Marquita S. Blades**, educational consultant,
POWARRful Teaching Strategies

EdTech Essentials is a celebration of the effective infusion of EdTech strategies into the classroom. Monica's love for sharing the best tools and the skills and protocols to ensure all students are successful is on full display in this new go-to resource for educators.

—**Al Thomas**, global educational speaker and consultant

EdTech Essentials removes all the clutter from what's out there and available for teachers and students. Monica shares tons of ideas that put students first in both face-to-face and online learning spaces. This book is filled with practical ideas, resources, classroom examples, and opportunities for reflection. Readers are sure to walk away with amazing ideas to help students become more productive, collaborative, and innovative. A must-read for every educator's professional toolbox!

—**Dr. Natasha Rachell**, director of instructional technology,
Atlanta Public Schools

EdTech Essentials provides an important action plan for teachers and schools implementing technology to facilitate learning and a critical lens on AI in education. This book includes indispensable examples, prompts, and teaching strategies across grade levels and diverse learning environments to help students and teachers navigate the digital landscape in school and beyond. Dr. Monica Burns guides readers through learning experiences that showcase positive digital citizenship and empower students to be collaborators and creators in our digital world.

—**Dr. Michele L. Haiken**, author and educator

EdTech Essentials, 2nd Edition

Also by Monica Burns

Tasks Before Apps: Designing Rigorous Learning in a Tech-Rich Classroom

Classroom Technology Tips (Quick Reference Guide)

Distance Learning Essentials (Quick Reference Guide)

Engaging Students in Reading All Types of Text (with Pam Allyn)
(Quick Reference Guide)

Using AI Chatbots to Enhance Planning and Instruction
(Quick Reference Guide)

EdTech Essentials

12 Strategies for Every Classroom in the Age of AI

2nd Edition

Monica Burns

Arlington, Virginia USA

Arlington, Virginia USA

2800 Shirlington Road, Suite 1001 • Arlington, VA 22206 USA
Phone: 800-933-2723 or 703-578-9600
Website: www.ascd.org • Email: member@ascd.org
Author guidelines: www.ascd.org/write

ISTE

2111 Wilson Boulevard, Suite 300 • Arlington, VA 22201 USA
Website: iste.org
ISTE® is a registered trademark of the International Society for Technology in Education.

Richard Culatta, *Chief Executive Officer;* Anthony Rebora, *Chief Content Officer;* Genny Ostertag, *Managing Director, Book Acquisitions & Editing;* Stephanie Bize, *Acquisitions Editor;* Mary Beth Nielsen, *Director, Book Editing;* Miriam Calderone, *Editor;* Thomas Lytle, *Creative Director;* Donald Ely, *Art Director;* Masie Chong, *Senior Graphic Designer;* Circle Graphics, *Typesetter;* Kelly Marshall, *Production Manager;* Shajuan Martin, *E-Publishing Specialist;* Kathryn Oliver, *Creative Project Manager*

PAPERBACK ISBN: 978-1-4166-3297-9   ASCD product #124028   n6/24
PDF EBOOK ISBN: 978-1-4166-3298-6; see Books in Print for other formats.
Quantity discounts are available: email programteam@ascd.org or call 800-933-2723, ext. 5773, or 703-575-5773. For desk copies, go to www.ascd.org/deskcopy.

Library of Congress Cataloging-in-Publication Data

Names: Burns, Monica, 1986- author.
Title: EdTech essentials : 12 strategies for every classroom in the age of AI / Monica Burns.
Other titles: Twelve strategies for every classroom in the age of artificial intelligence
Description: 2nd edition. | Arlington, Virginia : ASCD, [2024] | First edition published in 2021. |
   Includes bibliographical references and index.
Identifiers: LCCN 2024006129 (print) | LCCN 2024006130 (ebook) |
   ISBN 9781416632979 (paperback) | ISBN 9781416632986 (pdf)
Subjects: LCSH: Educational technology.
Classification: LCC LB1028.3 .B88 2024 (print) | LCC LB1028.3 (ebook) |
   DDC 371.33—dc23/eng/20240226
LC record available at https://lccn.loc.gov/2024006129
LC ebook record available at https://lccn.loc.gov/2024006130

33 32 31 30 29 28 27 26 25 24   1 2 3 4 5 6 7 8 9 10 11 12

To my mother: a teacher, mentor, and source of inspiration.

EdTech Essentials
12 Strategies for Every Classroom in the Age of AI, 2nd Edition

Introduction: EdTech Essentials Every Teacher
Should Consider in the Age of AI ——————————————— 1

1. **Navigate** Online Spaces Effectively ——————————— 7

2. **Curate** Resources to Support Every Student ——————— 23

3. **Generate** Ideas and Resources with Artificial Intelligence ————— 36

4. **Evaluate** Digital Content with an AI Mindset ——————— 47

5. **Explore** the World with Students ——————————— 54

6. **Collaborate** Across Digital Spaces ——————————— 67

7. **Create** Multimodal Artifacts of Learning ——————— 81

8. **Assess** to Check for Understanding and Pivot Instruction ————— 97

9. **Share** Student Creations in Big and Small Ways ——————— 107

10. **Connect** Students to Authentic Audiences ——————— 116

11. **Transfer** Skills Across Digital Spaces ——————— 125

12. **Plan** for Tech-Rich Learning Experiences ——————— 135

Appendix A: Essentials Versus Extras ——————————— 145

Appendix B: Resources for Taking Action ——————————— 151

Appendix C: Monica's Favorite Prompts to Use with Chatbots ————— 160

Appendix D: 100+ EdTech Tools and Resources for Teachers and Students —— 163

Appendix E: Additional Resources ——————————— 168

References ————————————————————————— 171

Index ——————————————————————————————— 175

About the Author ——————————————————————— 182

Study Guide ————————————————————————— 183

Introduction
EdTech Essentials Every Teacher Should Consider in the Age of AI

When we think of "the essentials," a few things come to mind, such as water, food, and shelter. Depending on whom you talk to, some might add Wi-Fi, a smartphone, or a favorite book to the list. Bringing it down to the basics, the Merriam-Webster Dictionary (n.d.) defines *essential* as follows:

- Of the utmost importance
- Something necessary, indispensable, or unavoidable

In today's environment, the ability to use technology effectively has become an *essential*. New technology has changed how we communicate, navigate the world, and create content—and we know more change is inevitable.

In this new edition of *EdTech Essentials*, we will examine the EdTech skills and strategies that are essential for all students if we want to prepare them to succeed in the digital world of today and tomorrow. In particular, the widespread use and easy availability of generative artificial intelligence (AI) has shifted our conversation on what every educator and student must understand about educational technology.

To be clear, the presence of AI in our lives isn't brand new. Many educators have used tools that employ adaptive AI to give students supporting resources as they answer review questions in an online tool, or to adjust to a student's needs in response to a baseline assessment. Generative AI is different. This type of artificial intelligence generates content and can include images, videos, music, and text. Instead of searching for pre-existing content, like using a search engine, generative AI *creates* content by combining information from a variety of sources.

This updated edition of *EdTech Essentials* is designed to help educators meet the needs of students in this changing landscape. The new edition you're looking at is a response to the proliferation of EdTech tools that leverage generative AI, the quick access we all have to chatbots, and the clear need for educators and students to understand the implications of AI. In 2023, ASCD and ISTE published my quick reference guide *Using AI Chatbots to Enhance Planning and Instruction* (Burns, 2023g) (accessible via the QR code). It provides a basic overview of what's possible with AI. This new edition of *EdTech Essentials* goes beyond the productivity and workflow focus of the quick reference guide with two new chapters ("**Generate** Ideas and Resources with Artificial Intelligence" and "**Evaluate** Digital Content with an AI Mindset") as well as a new appendix with suggested chatbot prompts to try. Throughout, I provide strategies that complement the original 10 essentials in this age of AI.

Using AI
Chatbots

Although many children have access to digital tools both inside and outside school, the quality of those experiences can vary greatly. Some students may listen to podcasts at home and understand the nuances of navigating audio content. Others may have heard the term *artificial intelligence* while not knowing what it means to "evaluate content with an AI mindset." (Having an AI mindset means understanding that content like images, text, or video might not be real but instead could have been generated with AI. We'll unpack this concept further in subsequent chapters.) If we truly believe the role of education in society is to prepare all children for success beyond the classroom, students must participate in meaningful, robust EdTech experiences. These kinds of experiences are necessary for every classroom, and in this book I share relevant stories, ideas, and action items. You'll find suggestions that are customizable for kindergarten through 12th grade, across all subject areas, and for classrooms with access to a variety of devices and programs.

The 12 Essentials

With so many options in the EdTech space, focusing on the essentials is key. To help center our conversation on what truly matters, I have narrowed the list to 12 essential skills and strategies, highlighting the roles of teachers and students in the age of AI. If you are familiar with my book *Tasks Before Apps: Designing Rigorous Learning in a Tech-Rich Classroom* (Burns, 2018), you know I firmly believe that with all things related to technology, *learning* must stay front and center, and digital tools should be used with intention.

I am often asked to speak on how to "make the most" of educational technology. Whether in a keynote presentation or in a casual conversation, I often bring it back to the worms—vermicomposting, to be more specific.

As a teacher in New York City, I started my career in a classroom with chalk, a chalkboard, and an overhead projector. Then iPads came on the scene, and I was lucky enough to pilot a one-to-one initiative with my 5th graders. So where do the worms come into play? In one corner of my classroom was a bright and shiny cart of new iPads, and in another was a bucket of worms—a compost bin, to be precise. There was no way we could ever drop a banana peel or an apple core into that iPad cart and expect anything good to come of it. But if we dropped these compostable items into our bin of worms, some serious change would take place. Both the cart and the bin had a purpose, and one wouldn't replace the other.

The intentional balance between digital and offline experiences requires thoughtful planning and an awareness of what students truly need to understand about leveraging technology effectively. In this book, I share 12 essential EdTech strategies. You can incorporate these essentials into the learning experiences you design for students over the course of the school year. They are flexible enough to inject into the content-rich work you already have planned and can complement your standards-aligned instructional goals:

- **Navigate** online spaces effectively.
- **Curate** resources to support every student.
- **Generate** ideas and resources with artificial intelligence.
- **Evaluate** digital content with an AI mindset.
- **Explore** the world with students.
- **Collaborate** across digital spaces.
- **Create** multimodal artifacts of learning.
- **Assess** to check for understanding and pivot instruction.
- **Share** student creations in big and small ways.
- **Connect** students to authentic audiences.
- **Transfer** skills across digital spaces.
- **Plan** for tech-rich learning experiences.

Although each of these essentials could itself fill a book, I have chosen to cover each one in a chapter, focusing on its main components. My intent is to provide information and tips you can put into action right away, as well as ideas to consider for your future planning. Each chapter includes an overview of the skill or strategy being discussed: why it is essential, connections to research, classroom examples for all grade levels, websites and mobile apps to help build your EdTech tool belt, and guiding questions to use for your individual planning and reflection or when planning new learning experiences with colleagues.

Connecting with the ISTE Standards

These 12 essentials also connect to the ISTE Standards. ISTE represents educators who are passionate about thoughtful technology integration, and I have learned much from attending and presenting at ISTE's Annual Conference for the past decade. The ISTE Standards "provide the competencies for learning, teaching and leading with technology, and are a comprehensive road map for the effective use of technology in schools worldwide. Grounded in learning science research and based on practitioner experience, the ISTE Standards ensure that using technology for learning creates high-impact, sustainable, scalable and equitable learning experiences for all learners." An overview of each section of the standards follows.

ISTE Student Standards: "Today's students must be prepared to thrive in an evolving technological landscape. The student section of the ISTE Standards is designed to empower student voice and ensure that learning is a student-driven process" (ISTE, 2016).

ISTE Educator Standards: "The educator section of the ISTE Standards provides a road map to helping students become empowered learners. These standards will deepen your practice, promote collaboration with peers, challenge you to rethink traditional approaches and help you prepare students to drive their own learning" (ISTE, 2017).

ISTE Education Leader Standards: "The education leaders section of the ISTE Standards supports the implementation of both the student and educator sections of ISTE Standards by targeting the knowledge and behaviors required for leaders to empower teachers and boost student learning. This section is focused on equity, digital citizenship, visioneering, team and systems building, continuous improvement and professional growth" (ISTE, 2018).

ISTE Coaching Standards: "The coaches section of the ISTE Standards illustrates the characteristics, activities, philosophies and mindsets of today's instructional technology coaches. Because coaches have a unique role as capacity builders and implementation experts, these standards guide coaches in ensuring that learning with technology is high impact, sustainable, scalable and equitable for all" (ISTE, 2020).

Throughout the book, you will find strategies and examples that relate to these standards at the indicator level. You can learn more about ISTE and the ISTE Standards at https://iste.org/standards (or scan the QR code).

ISTE
Standards

Resources to Support Your EdTech Journey

At the end of the book, you will find resources to help you design and implement learning experiences for students that take these essentials into account. Appendix A summarizes some of the big ideas from each chapter to help you prioritize how to address the EdTech essentials in your own learning environment. Appendix B provides forms to help you set goals, assess your progress, and build your EdTech tool belt. These forms are also available for download at https://www.ascd.org/edtech-essentials-resources (or scan the QR code). In the new Appendix C ("Monica's Favorite Prompts to Use with Chatbots"), you'll find a handful of prompts I encourage you to try out as you explore generative AI. Appendix D is a roundup of popular EdTech tools to complement the suggestions you find in each chapter. The list has been updated for this edition and reorganized by category or purpose of tool. Some of the tools listed are free, while some have a price tag; some are from companies I have worked closely with, and others are from companies that are new on the scene. In the new Appendix E, you'll find an extensive collection of further resources—books, websites, learning opportunities, and more—that will help you extend your exploration into various EdTech topics, such as digital citizenship and AI. Finally, you'll find a study guide to further your own exploration of the concepts in this book or to support a book club or learning community at your school. You can download a PDF version of the study guide at https://classtechtips.com/studyguide (or scan the QR code).

EdTech Essentials Resources

Study Guide

Whether you have been teaching for a few years or a few decades, you know every school year is different. In the same way you customize learning experiences for each group of students you work with, you can take the ideas I share and make them your own. As an educator, you are the content expert, and you know your students (and colleagues) best. My role is to help make EdTech easier so you can integrate digital tools into your classrooms with intention while taking advantage of all EdTech has to offer.

Follow along with my EdTech adventures:

- Class Tech Tips Blog with weekly updates: ClassTechTips.com/blog
- *Easy EdTech Podcast* with new episodes on Tuesdays: ClassTechTips.com/podcast
- Free Monday newsletter with a weekly EdTech roundup: ClassTechTips.com/newsletter
- Search for @ClassTechTips on your favorite social media platform (including Instagram, Pinterest, and more).

1

Navigate Online Spaces Effectively

handle, maneuver, operate, journey, transverse, pass, manage

Whether it is early in the morning or late at night, there is a good chance you have already navigated many online spaces in the few or many hours since you arose this morning. Did you scroll through a blog post or listen to a podcast episode? Did you open up a search engine to find an answer to a question? You and your students have likely clicked, saved, played, and shared across online spaces in the past 24 hours.

Given the prevalence of online activity in everyday life, students should know how to find what they are looking for and how to make the most of the information available to them online. This capability includes taking advantage of every feature within a website or mobile app, evaluating and synthesizing the seemingly endless amount of content available online, and tackling logistical challenges (like what button to press to find what they need) along the way.

It may seem that the children in our lives can pick up a device and immediately find a popular YouTube channel or viral video on TikTok. However, we know access to devices—and quality experiences with technology—can vary greatly. All students need to be able to **navigate** online spaces effectively. In this chapter, we examine what navigating online spaces entails, why it is important, and how we can set up learning experiences to help students cultivate this essential skill.

Why Is This Essential?

Whether we are traversing the subway system in New York City or driving a car above ground, navigation skills are critical when we enter any new or familiar physical space. The same holds true when students move around an online space.

In this book, I use *online spaces* as an all-encompassing term to describe the content and communication channels students can access online. Online spaces can include websites with articles and blog posts, video platforms with clips and tutorials, and mobile apps on a smartphone or tablet that present information to students in multimedia formats. These spaces have evolved over time, and the company names and user interfaces might have changed, too.

There are more spaces to consume online content than ever before. Names such as YouTube, TikTok, and Spotify have entered the lexicon of anyone with access to a digital device. People watch more than one billion hours of video on YouTube each day (YouTube, n.d.); TikTok users spend an average of almost an hour viewing content each day (Mohsin, 2020); and Spotify hosts more than five million podcast titles (Spotify, n.d.)—including my *Easy EdTech Podcast* and plenty of narrative and informational content designed for students, educators, and the market at large.

ISTE Student Standard Indicator 1.1.d, Technology Operations, states, "Students understand the fundamental concepts of technology operations; demonstrate the ability to choose, use and troubleshoot current technologies; and are able to transfer their knowledge to explore emerging technologies."

Navigating online spaces effectively is clearly an essential skill. Moreover, it is directly tied to media literacy and is a component of media literacy education. The National Association for Media Literacy Education (NAMLE) defines *media literacy education* in terms of the skills and knowledge a student needs to "access, analyze, evaluate, create, and act" using all forms of communication. It defines *media* as "digital media, computers, video games, radio, television, mobile media, print, and communication technologies that we have not even dreamed of yet" (NAMLE, n.d.).

When and how you introduce navigational skills—and the opportunities you provide to students to put them into action—will vary across grade levels and subject areas. However, one thing is certain: students of all ages should have ample opportunity to practice navigational skills.

Exploring Digital Features

Consumers are not just part of the food chain or the supply chain—even if we feel like we're devouring content with the ferocity of an apex predator. As much as I love an example using sharks or dinosaurs, in this chapter, the all-encompassing term *consumer* includes people (like you, me, and our students) who read, view, and listen to content in online spaces.

As consumers of online content, students will come across key features—text, links, images, audio, and video—regardless of the device in their hand or on their desk. Later in the chapter, we discuss how to model navigating online spaces with these features in mind. For now, let's consider when they might appear on a student's screen.

Text

Text in an online space can be paragraphs in a news article or chapters in an ebook that mirror the text students consume in print materials. Students might also find text in shorter form, such as a caption on a photograph, a summary of a podcast episode, or a list of recommended resources that accompanies a tutorial video. This text could include an option to tap on a word and see a definition or hear how it is pronounced. A word, phrase, or sentence might be underlined to indicate it is linked to another piece of content.

Links

Links appear throughout online spaces and connect students to content hosted on a separate page. A link could take users to another resource created by the same organization or publication, such as when an online magazine mentions an event and provides

Embedded Items

Online spaces are full of interactive items that give users access to extra content. A web designer or an app developer might insert an interactive item to connect a reader to other content relevant to the topic. The goal of this embedded item, sometimes called a widget, is to add value, make a connection, or provide additional information. For example, in an online newspaper article about an event in Cairo, you might find an embedded item for Google Maps where a reader can tap and explore a map of Cairo as a way to extend the reading experience. In addition to interactive maps, examples of embedded items include the following:

- Video clips from a player like YouTube or Vimeo

- Timers or countdown clocks to promote an event

- Slideshows of pictures for viewers to scroll through

- Forms to collect information or a widget for adding comments

a link to one of its own articles covering that event. A link could also take readers to another website chosen by the creator of the original resource. When you are navigating an online space, it may be unclear how well a piece of linked content is vetted, so you may need to review the quality and authority of that secondary source.

Images

Photographs and illustrations appear throughout online spaces, whether students are scrolling through Instagram or opening up a Wikipedia entry. Similar to the pictures in a textbook or another piece of informational text, both the visual on the page and the accompanying caption provide information. In the same way students learn about using pictures when reading a book, students who navigate online spaces view images as sources of potentially valuable information. Artificial intelligence tools can generate photorealistic images that depict a notable figure or well-known space inaccurately. Some of these images may have clear disclosures stating that the image was made with the help of AI, and others may have no attribution.

> **Microblogging**
>
> In online spaces such as Instagram, where images are the core content on the page, captions can hold more value than they do when accompanying pictures in traditional text-based forms of content like newspaper articles. The term *microblogging* is often associated with lengthy captions found in social media posts that provide a narrative or detailed information on a subject.

Audio

Audio content can appear in short and long form as both a free and a paid resource. Podcasts are generally available for free through a podcast player (like Apple Podcasts, Google Podcasts, or Spotify). You might listen to podcasts through a player embedded on the website of the podcast host or company behind a podcast. Audio content can include ebooks that readers access on a web browser or through a device like an ereader or tablet (e.g., Kindle). You might also encounter audio content on a web page, such as an audio recording accompanying an article that gives you the option to press play and hear content read aloud.

Video

Although you and I might remember the days of rolling a television cart into a classroom, the amount of video students consume and the way they access this content have changed greatly in the last few decades. Video content is available on multiple platforms, and Google's search engine even includes the option to respond to a search query with a list of videos instead of a list of websites. You can find videos embedded in websites in addition to native video platforms like YouTube and Vimeo. Video content extends beyond these hosting sites and into social spaces such as Instagram, TikTok, and Facebook, where it is often posted with captions and links.

Guiding Students' Online Search Experiences

Text, links, images, audio, and video are some of the key content types and features students will come across in online spaces. Navigating online spaces to search for information applies to all subject areas. For example, students might look for the exact date of a historical event as they create a timeline in a social studies classroom or seek contact information for a professor at a local university so they can send a question related to a chemistry experiment. Let's explore how you can create, support, and extend learning experiences that involve searching online. We'll start by examining traditional keyword searches and finish with tips for searching for information using prompts with chatbots and generative AI.

Ensuring Accessibility

Navigating online spaces may present specific challenges for students who require additional support using digital tools. To make sure you are creating equitable spaces for students, review the needs of your students with accessibility in mind. You may want to explore these three resources that provide product-specific information on how to best support all learners:

- Immersive Reader from Microsoft: https://www.microsoft.com/en-us/education/products/learning-tools

- Chromebook Accessibility Overview: https://edu.google.com/why-google/accessibility/chromebooks-accessibility

- Apple Accessibility Overview: https://www.apple.com/accessibility

Keyword Searches

To create keyword search–related learning experiences for students, first identify what information you would like them to collect. This could include information related to a simple question with a correct/incorrect answer or something more complex and open-ended. Although at times you will want students to search more broadly, such as when you want them to explore a large topic and choose a subtopic to research, in this case we are talking about setting a narrow purpose so that students go off on a specific mission.

As you create online search experiences, you might work together as a whole class or have students search independently or with a partner.

To establish a clear purpose for online searches, you can use the following statements in your planning and in your discussion with students:

- Today we will investigate . . .
- We might use keyword search terms such as . . .
- We will collect our findings by . . .

We don't know what we don't know

Our intentions when searching online can vary from finding a quick answer to a question to researching a complex topic. *Simple* searches are useful in many instances, but sometimes you will want students to go off on a *deep-dive* search to identify a question or topic they would like to explore further. In the same way that "we don't know what we don't know," your students can benefit from searches that provide context for future learning experiences and research opportunities.

In a 1st grade classroom, you might share QR codes students can scan to access links to a few short video clips. They can watch the clips to help them decide which animal they would like to research before reading an informational text or starting a social studies unit on an area of the world where an endangered species lives. In a high school classroom, you might send students off with a big idea such as "climate change" and then allow time for them to search broadly. Students can gather ideas on subtopics to investigate with more purpose during a unit on persuasive writing or environmental science. Here are some examples of *simple* searches and *deep-dive* searches:

- 1st grade—*Simple:* How much rain fell last summer? *Deep dive:* Why does it rain more in one state than in another?
- 4th grade—*Simple:* What year did Arizona become a state? *Deep dive:* Why did Arizona gain statehood after the 13 colonies?

Introducing Chatbot Queries to Students

Traditional keyword searches are just one way students can locate information in online spaces. Although chatbot tools like ChatGPT are not, at the time of publication, compliant with the Children's Online Privacy Protection Act of 1998 (COPPA)–which "imposes certain requirements on operators of websites or online services directed to children under 13 years of age, and on operators of other websites or online services that have actual knowledge that they are collecting personal information online from a child under 13 years of age"–this type of technology is bound to increase in popularity. Even if you do not plan to have students open up a chatbot themselves, you might demonstrate how this technology works. To illustrate, you might share the results of a keyword search (e.g., "red fruits") and the output of a chatbot (e.g., "Make a list of red fruits") for students to compare and contrast. Alternatively, you might share the output of a chatbot (e.g., "Explain the difference between fruits and vegetables") and ask students to find sources to support these findings.

- 11th grade—*Simple:* What country is Jane Austen from? *Deep dive:* What factors in Jane Austen's life influenced the themes of her novels? (Burns, 2018, p. 50)

ISTE Educator Standard Indicator 2.6.a, Foster Student Ownership of Learning, asks educators to "Foster a culture where students take ownership of their learning goals and outcomes in both independent and group settings." As you work to support students' navigation of digital spaces, you can offer resources such as graphic organizers and model strategies with a think aloud that help students build independence in online spaces.

Support

In addition to setting a clear purpose and modeling, you can provide other supports to help students stay on task. Working with a partner, periodic check-ins, and turn-and-talks can help students stay accountable during an online learning experience. Other options include engaging in a whole-group discussion in the middle of a lesson or adding an exit ticket or share-out at the end of a lesson allowing students to post an update on their progress.

Establishing clear expectations and modeling for students will also set them up for success as they practice navigating online spaces. Although we all know how easy it is to get distracted in online spaces—I have many tabs open on my Chrome browser right now—setting and sharing a clear purpose for time spent online will help students stay on track. When modeling for students, you might "think aloud" to demonstrate what you are thinking as you move through an online space, saying something like "This link looks interesting, but it is not going to help me find the answer to my question" or "I love videos like this, and maybe I'll watch it later, but right now, it is not going to help me accomplish my goal."

What Is a "Think Aloud"?

Molly Ness, author of *Think Big with Think Alouds, Grades K–5* (2018b), describes this tactic as a powerful comprehension strategy. In an article written for *We Are Teachers,* she comments on the observations of a teacher conducting a reading lesson and explains how "throughout her read-aloud, this teacher will stop to ask questions, make observations, and think deeply about the story" (Ness, 2018a). The same process can happen as students listen to their teachers share their thinking while they tackle a math problem, examine a primary source document, or decide if a YouTube video comes from a trusted source. For example, you might "think aloud" while searching for information as you model for students which decisions you make as you look for an answer to a question.

There are tools that help students focus on a single task and help them avoid distractions when working online. You can model one of these tools for students to try when working independently, or share them with your class to help everyone stay focused on a task:

- Brain.fm: music you can stream on any device designed to help listeners focus
- Flora: an app and Chrome extension where users set an amount of time to focus on a task and watch a plant grow if they avoid distractions
- Calm: a platform to access music designed to improve focus on a task

Here are a few other things you can do to support your students' keyword searches:

- Share keyword search strategies, such as using a phrase instead of a complete sentence or question.
- Brainstorm potential keywords and search terms with students before sending them off to work independently or with a partner.
- Post common search queries for your topic so students do not have to worry about spelling errors, which can lead to unhelpful results or frustration.
- If the results of their search queries are not helping them find useful information on the topic, remind students to check for misspellings, or encourage them to try a new keyword or phrase.
- Inform students about voice-to-text search options, which are available on many websites and mobile apps, and model how to conduct a voice-to-text search and how to address any errors with the dictation technology. *Note: these tools will often require students to grant the tool permission to use their device's microphone.*
- Introduce students to advanced search options to help them find a specific type of result or file. For example, Google and YouTube have advanced search options to let users search for content published in the last few months or the previous year. Advanced search features are often hidden next to the search bar; look for the word *Filters* or *Tools* to help you refine your searches.

Extend

The amount of time you allocate for students to navigate online spaces will depend on the task. To extend these experiences and provide more opportunities for exploration, you can have students participate in activities such as a "scavenger hunt" that asks them to find the answers to a series of questions. If you find yourself in a teachable moment where a student asks a question you cannot answer yourself, you might ask the class to search for the answer to the question. Although you might not pause your planned instruction that very moment, you can revisit the question to model an online search or ask students to find the answer later.

Finding Answers with Chatbots

The widespread adoption of generative artificial intelligence has shifted the way we think about traditional searches. Instead of hearing someone use *Google* as a verb when they say, "Let's Google the answer . . . ," you might now hear someone say, "I asked ChatGPT to find the answer." In Chapter 3, we'll examine strategies educators can use to generate instructional content with the help of chatbot technology, and in Chapter 4, we'll look at ways to support students as they evaluate content created with generative AI. For the purpose of this chapter, it is essential for students to understand how to navigate online searches when chatbots present a viable option for locating information.

As mentioned previously, popular chatbot technology like ChatGPT, Claude, and Gemini are not designed for students to use in a school setting at this time. Keeping this in mind, you might model strategies for conducting queries with a chatbot in preparation for a time when students will navigate these tools independently inside a classroom setting or out of the classroom with a family member's support. You can customize the following four activities for your group of students, changing the subject matter and discussion goals as needed:

- *Compare and contrast:* have students review the results you received from a traditional keyword search and the results of your

A Search Activity

You might not expect Instagram to be a source for inspiration, but if you follow educators on this social media platform, you will find many who share ideas and tips with their followers. I first came across this activity from fellow Apple Distinguished Educator Larry Reiff while scrolling through Instagram. To help students practice using online tools, he shares prompts that require them to think critically and combine information from various sources to find the answer. For example, he gave them this challenge: "Add up all of the digits of the zip code for the town where the physicist who directed the Manhattan Project received his undergraduate degree." Students have to work backward and search for smaller pieces of information to help them build toward the answer.

Primary Sources in a Digital World

We often think of the phrase *primary source* as describing something such as an artifact in a museum. Although primary sources can be tangible—for example, a letter or an entry in a journal you can hold in your hand—many are digital. Email correspondence, blog posts, and *vlogs* (blog entries in video format) fall into this category, too.

chatbot query, comparing and contrasting the results. Ask them to share their thoughts in a graphic organizer or turn-and-talk to a partner.

- *Provide feedback:* share the output from a chatbot and have students provide feedback on the response. They can write down what important information is missing or what they would have expected to see based on the query.
- *Fact-check:* provide the output of a query for students to fact-check. They can practice their keyword searches to "fact-check" the results and evaluate whether the response produced by the chatbot is accurate.
- *Rewrite the prompt:* share with students your intended output, the actual output from the chatbot, and the prompt you used. Ask them to rewrite the prompt to better align with your intended output to help you receive a stronger response.

There are a few factors that make a keyword search different from using a chatbot to find answers to a question. A keyword search can provide a quick answer to a simple question with only one correct response (e.g., "year Declaration of Independence signed"). Or it can provide a list of resources a student can use when researching a topic (e.g., "How to join the Space Force"). A chatbot will respond to a query in a format it thinks will be helpful, like a list, or in a format you ask for, like a table. It will respond to deep-dive questions by synthesizing information from a variety of sources. Some chatbots provide a link to the source material for their response, whereas others do not. As we'll explore more in Chapters 3 and 4, the output of a chatbot may be inaccurate or biased. Students—and educators—who use a chatbot to search for information need to take these factors into consideration when reviewing responses in the same way they review the recommended resources from a search engine like Google or Bing.

Figure 1.1 shows some specific examples at various grade levels.

Organizing Information

Students encounter a lot of information as they navigate online spaces. There may be times when they are diligently collecting information for a research project, and other times when they simply want to keep track of links to a video, podcast episode, or blog post to revisit at a later date.

FIGURE 1.1

Cross-Curricular Examples of Keyword Searches and Chatbot Prompts

Prompt	Grade Level			
	Early Elementary	**Upper Elementary**	**Middle School**	**High School**
Today we will investigate . . .	What types of food a polar bear eats.	How the winter weather is different in Minnesota and Alabama.	The life and works of Sandra Cisneros.	Different methods for solving quadratic equations.
We might use search terms such as . . .	"Polar bear diet." "Foods polar bears eat."	"Minnesota weather in January." "Average temperatures in Alabama."	"Sandra Cisneros biography." "Sandra Cisneros books."	"Ways to solve quadratic equations." "Strategies for solving quadratic equations."
[A teacher might submit a prompt to a chatbot such as . . .]	"Make a list of foods a polar bear eats." "Compare and contrast what a polar bear eats and what a human eats on a given day."	"Make a table with the average precipitation and temperature for the last 10 years for Minnesota and Alabama." "Write a paragraph that describes the way the weather in Minnesota and Alabama is most similar in the winter months."	"Provide a list of Sandra Cisneros publications with available sales numbers." "Make a list of interview questions for the author Sandra Cisneros."	"Explain the steps to solve this problem [add specific problem]." "Make a list of scenarios where someone would use a quadratic equation."
We will organize our findings by . . .	Sharing what we are learning via video on our class Seesaw page.	Adding the information to a Google Doc.	Creating a mind map with color-coded information based on different categories.	Sharing the video tutorial we find most useful in our class discussion forum.

Although some students, especially in middle or high school, may have a system for remembering where they found information, teaching students strategies for organizing information is an important part of helping them learn how to navigate online spaces effectively.

In the past, we might have used spiral notebooks or index cards to organize information when researching a topic. Organizing links, annotations, notes, and files using digital tools is very different from physically moving index cards to place notes into categories, or high-lighting and color-coding research in a physical notebook. Digital tools enable students to organize information in myriad ways. They can keep track of their notes and ideas by typing or using *voice-to-text* (as well as some video recording options) into popular spaces like Google Docs. Students can also add links by *copy-and-pasting* URLs to websites they have visited to a space like Microsoft OneNote. If students have a file to add to their notes, they can also copy-and-paste a link to that file (such as a Google Drive or Dropbox link) or upload the file itself to a folder.

Strategies for organizing digital notes include graphic organizers, interactive documents, and journaling. Let's take a brief look at each of these three categories.

Graphic Organizers

A graphic organizer is a visual representation of information. Students can organize information visually using a premade or static graphic organizer, using a dynamic or customizable graphic organizer, or in a blank space where they use a variety of elements to organize information in any way they choose, like a mind map. Modeling, providing support, and offering examples are important steps in helping students get started. Using an open-ended tool—one that is not task-specific and can be used for various purposes—is a great choice. Let's explore three types of graphic organizers:

- A **static graphic organizer** is similar to a PDF of a worksheet where students can make annotations using digital tools but are working within specific constraints. This is a great way to take a traditional resource and add a digital layer. Students can add text boxes, draw in a space, or even record voice notes. By accessing a static graphic organizer in a digital space (instead of printing it out on a piece of paper), your goal should be to leverage digital features that increase access and engagement for students. *Envision: A PDF added to a space like Seesaw for 2nd graders to have the option to record voice notes or add text boxes as they compare and contrast the characters from a story.*
- A **dynamic graphic organizer** provides a baseline or template for students that they can use as is or customize. This is a great way to give students support and flexibility at the same time. *Envision:*

Providing students access to a tool like Book Creator with their built-in timeline graphic organizers. Students can move, delete, and add elements on the premade page to customize the graphic organizer and make it their own.

- A **mind map** is a type of graphic organizer where students can add shapes, lines, and arrows to organize information. Mind maps use some of the same principles of traditional graphic organizers but provide more flexibility for organization. This can make them a more versatile option than a one-size-fits-all approach, but the blank space may feel intimidating to students who crave more structure. Students will benefit from seeing examples and receiving feedback on how to use such a space. *Envision: Students use a space like FigJam or Google Drawings to organize information for a research project. They add links and images alongside traditional color-coding and text.*

Interactive Documents

Unlike organizing notes on a sheet of paper or in a notebook, an interactive document enables students to connect information from multiple places and make it accessible by clicking on a link. Students can add notes along with any resources they have found and quickly reorganize information with a copy-and-paste. One benefit of interactive documents is the option to share with multiple users for collaboration, commenting, and feedback. This type of document might include *hyperlinks,* which connect users to a different document or to a specific place within the document they are currently using. Here are some examples of tools you can use for interactive documents:

- Microsoft Word
- Google Docs
- Canva Docs
- Pages

Definitions

Open-ended tool: a versatile digital tool that is not limited to one prescribed use

Hyperlink: a link that connects two documents or parts of a document; often used in documents with a table of contents or multiple elements

Reading Online Text

Pam Allyn and I (Allyn & Burns, 2021) wrote a quick reference guide titled *Engaging Students in Reading All Types of Text* (scan the QR code). This guide includes tips for extending reading experiences and ways to help students interact with online text.

Engaging Students in Reading All Types of Text

Pam was also a guest on my (2023h) *Easy EdTech Podcast* (to listen, scan the QR code).

Easy EdTech Podcast: 235

How to Help Students Become Tech-Savvy

Dr. Cassidy Puckett (2022) shares five learning habits for students in her book *Redefining Geek: Bias and the Five Hidden Habits of Tech-Savvy Teens*. These include the technology-specific habits of *design logic* and *efficiencies*. Puckett describes *design logic* as a habit that "focuses more centrally on the learning process, the changing nature of technological tools, and what the learner brings to the table" (p. 89). The habit of *efficiencies* includes "awareness that software and hardware often (but not always) have shorter ways of accomplishing tasks . . . thinking about how to find these shorter pathways to make work and learning faster . . . [and] the behavior of trying out and practicing these efficient ways of accomplishing tasks" (p. 96). Both these habits connect to the essential skill of navigating digital spaces effectively. Cassidy was also a guest on my (2022d) *Easy EdTech Podcast* (to listen, scan the QR code).

Easy EdTech Podcast: 168

Journaling

Digital journals provide multiple ways for students to build upon their learning over time. They are similar to a traditional journal but are equipped with a variety of tools students can use to add an update, including capabilities such as voice-to-text, audio and video recording, and insertion of links. Journaling with digital tools provides more access points for students, enabling them to choose how to interact with content and how they would like to share their learning experiences. Digital journals can also make it easier for teachers to check on a student's progress, a topic we will explore further in our discussion of assessment in Chapter 8. Here are some examples of tools you can use for journaling:

- Seesaw
- Book Creator
- Adobe Express
- Google Slides

Synthesizing Information

Students can create a variety of products to share what they have learned, from book trailers to interactive science reports. We will explore this topic of student creations in more detail in Chapter 7. For now, let's consider how creating something requires students to take information they have gathered from different places and pull it all together—to synthesize. What does this look like in online spaces?

In an early-elementary classroom, students may watch a video and hear a book about ocean creatures read aloud. Then they may make a list or draw a picture of all the things they now know about sharks. Students can make an audio recording of their digital list or snap a picture of their illustration using a digital journaling tool and record their voice to explain their thinking.

In an upper-elementary classroom, students may read a selection of online encyclopedia entries and watch a short documentary on the

Dust Bowl. Then they may create a mind map, independently or with a partner, using an online whiteboard space to explain the who, what, when, where, why, and how of the event. Using color-coding and links to additional resources, students can organize everything they have learned into one space.

In a middle school classroom, students may research the effect wearing a seatbelt has on injuries caused by a car accident. They may interview a local emergency room doctor via Zoom or Google Meet, watch a series of public service announcements posted on YouTube, and review data collected by a safety organization and posted to its public website. Students can then create an interactive document to organize the information they have collected (and the associated links to additional information) into different categories.

In a high school classroom, students may create an interactive document to organize their research on a topic related to a community action project. They can create a table with their research findings in Microsoft Word or Google Docs and add their own thinking in a column beside their research. Students can insert links within the document to create a table of contents and record audio notes as they gather information and address lingering questions. By leaving comments in the document or tagging other classmates to ask for feedback or suggestions, students can use this space to work collaboratively, as well.

Addressing Logistics

To navigate online spaces effectively and use the strategies shared in this chapter, students need basic computing skills. These strategies are sometimes taught in isolation in a computer lab or technology class. However, there are moments throughout the school day when you can model a strategy or teach it explicitly in the context of your curriculum and content-area goals.

Using Shortcuts as You Navigate Digital Spaces

One navigational strategy already present in many educators' practice is the use of keyboard shortcuts (also referred to as *hotkeys*). For example, you might use shortcuts to copy and paste by selecting the text you want to copy and pressing Ctrl+C on your keyboard. Then you instinctively place your cursor where you want to paste the copied text and press Ctrl+V. Once keyboard shortcuts become part of your everyday practice, they can save you lots of time. For example, they are helpful for efficiently inserting links, notes, or additional content in interactive documents and opening or closing tabs so you can move from one part of your screen to another. They can also help students quickly annotate their work. If you are using a program or online tool frequently with students, you can introduce these shortcuts to help them understand how there are faster, more efficient ways to navigate digital spaces.

How can you find out which shortcuts are available for popular tools?

- Find the FAQ page on the website of your favorite tool.
- Search for "keyboard shortcuts for [name of tool]" in a search engine like Google.
- Ask colleagues to share their favorite keyboard shortcut at the start of your next faculty meeting.

There are a variety of schools of thought on direct keyboarding instruction. I often compare the situation to the need to understand times tables in order to complete complex math problems quickly and efficiently. We may reach a point in the future where voice-to-text replaces the need for keyboarding, but as the second edition of *EdTech Essentials* goes to press, we are still not there. Ignoring the need for keyboard practice would be impractical, and just like the example of teaching students times tables, there are different ways to get there. You may want to explore a comprehensive keyboarding program aligned to the needs of your students.

Some students can pick up a new device and instantly sense how to use every feature and find every button. However, we know this is not the case for all students, and even those who have ample experience with digital tools might not understand the specific classroom use you have in mind. Alongside keyboarding instruction, helping students understand how to use trackpads, touchscreens, and cameras is necessary for their success in navigating online spaces. In Chapter 11, we will discuss helping students develop skills in areas such as problem solving and troubleshooting that will transfer across devices and platforms. When introducing or reviewing device features with students, modeling and reminding them of how to maneuver within a particular device is absolutely necessary.

Final Thoughts

Similar to the way you might teach vocabulary words in context, you can introduce essential EdTech strategies like *navigate* within the content taught across grade levels and subject areas. Instead of planning to teach a lesson with a teaching point such as "Students will be able to click on a link" or "Students will be able to take pictures with their tablet," incorporate these essential EdTech experiences into content you are already teaching. Demonstrating how navigating online spaces is not an isolated activity but an integral part of interacting with technology in general can reinforce the skills you want students to build.

2

Curate Resources to Support Every Student

select, pull together, sift through, locate, sort, organize, prioritize, share, choose

Online spaces can feel noisy at times, with notifications popping up on our screens, alerts continually beeping, and a plethora of content just a few clicks away. From videos to news articles, mobile apps, and social media platforms, the digital world is a busy place. We want students to navigate these spaces and develop transferable skills that help them adapt to current and future innovations in technology. Building student independence, modeling strategies for evaluating content, and sending students out to navigate online spaces is only part of the process.

As educators, we can **curate** resources that connect to curriculum goals while supporting the needs of all students. By thoughtfully pulling together content throughout the school year, we can differentiate the resources shared with students to meet everyone's needs. In this chapter, we examine strategies to help you select, organize, and distribute online resources with students. Traditional curation strategies—particularly when supported by AI tools—can help you ensure students have access to a wide variety of supplemental resources this school year.

Why Is This Essential?

Selecting "just right" resources for students is an essential practice for educators to help make sure the needs of all students are addressed. As you select resources for an entire class, for small groups of students, or for individuals, you have an opportunity to place relevant, even personalized resources in their hands. This curation is essential because it tunes out the noise generated by a long list of materials and narrows the focus for students. Instead of sending them to a search engine, you can share videos, articles, short text items, tutorials, and more, chosen strategically to address the specific student needs you have identified.

How is the practice of curating resources related to differentiation? In *How to Differentiate Instruction in Academically Diverse Classrooms,* Carol Ann Tomlinson (2017) states, "A differentiated classroom provides different avenues to acquiring content, to processing or making sense of ideas, and to developing products so that each student can learn effectively" (p. 1). Curating resources is part of the puzzle of creating a differentiated learning environment. Although there are resources teachers might share with every student in a classroom, thoughtful curation addresses the needs of each student by sharing handpicked resources with them.

A purposeful practice of curating digital resources means you are attentive to content, representation, and student interest. All three of these are part of a high-quality plan to place "just right" resources in front of students. To develop such a plan, you can ask the following questions:

- *Content:* Do the materials address the big ideas and narrower subtopics you want students to understand?
- *Representation:* Do students see themselves in the resources you have chosen? Do these resources help them place themselves in the content and see course material as relevant?
- *Student interest:* Have you identified subtopics or related content areas that students have shown an interest in learning more about?

Curating Strong Resources

In 2020, the *New York Times* published an article titled "Everyone's a Curator Now." In it, reporter Lou Stoppard quotes Hans-Ulrich Obrist, the artistic director of Serpentine Galleries in London, who states, "I see a curator as a catalyst, generator, and motivator."

When I use the term *curation,* I cannot help but think of a museum. Museum curators *select* which pieces to feature in an upcoming exhibit. They *organize* each piece so it follows a clear pathway in telling a story. Instead of opening up the doors to the basement of a museum and having visitors sift through all the artwork and artifacts (although this sounds like a fun field trip!), they *prioritize* what appears on the walls and in the display cases of an exhibit. As an educator, you are a curator who selects, organizes, and prioritizes which resources to share with students.

Categories of Content

To determine the best resources for students, let's first consider several core categories of digital content: video, text, images, graphics, audio, and files. Each offers a benefit.

Video. From high-quality hour-long documentaries to 30-second viral clips, online video content can vary greatly. A creator can upload a video to a video-sharing platform, such as YouTube or Vimeo. Students and teachers with a smartphone or computer can access that video and share a link to it for someone else to view. A video creator can establish sharing settings that may or may not include the ability to download a video for offline use; often videos must be played from a website or an app with an internet connection.

Text. Content in this category can include news articles, encyclopedia entries, interviews, or even blog posts. These resources are typically presented alongside other media, such as images with captions or embedded video and audio. These pieces of content vary in length and ease of navigation. Students may want to view text content using the "Reader View" option of their web browser. This removes extra items such as advertisements and sidebars from a web page to eliminate distraction and visual clutter for readers of any age.

Images. Photographs or still images can present information to students and illustrate ideas. You might use this content to supplement a reading or listening experience in a classroom. In online spaces, images are sometimes organized in slideshows or collections.

Graphics. Another visual format is graphics, which can present information with images, icons, and text. An infographic uses visuals

Video Search Tips

YouTube and other platforms with video content can feel like crowded spaces. When searching for videos in a space like YouTube, you can take advantage of the following features to help you sort through the content:

- *Channel:* a dedicated space established by an organization so it can post its videos in one place
- *Playlist:* a list created by a user (you or someone else) to organize favorite videos into a collection
- *Advanced search:* an option for sorting keyword search results by video quality, length, file type, and more

Easy EdTech Podcast

Check out Episode 128 of my (2021) *Easy EdTech Podcast* to learn about "Useful Tips for Finding Podcasts to Enhance Content with Jeff Glade" (to listen, scan the QR code). In this popular episode, educator and podcast enthusiast Jeff Glade discusses ways to use podcasts in the classroom and how this practice can open the world to students of all ages. You'll also hear about high-quality, student-friendly podcasts and activities you can try out right away.

Easy EdTech Podcast: 128

to illustrate data. Students may be familiar with seeing graphical representations of information shared on social media.

Audio. Audio-only content has become increasingly popular, given the recent rise in the number of podcasts available to download or stream. Podcast episodes can have an individual focus or be part of an ongoing series. They are typically available to download for offline listening, and users can stream them from a website or listen on a dedicated mobile app for podcasts like Spotify, Apple Podcasts, or Overcast. Many podcasts give listeners access to a transcript of the episode, too. In addition to podcasts, audio content may include blog posts or text-based content with an option for students to listen to it as it is read aloud.

Files. A computer file basically takes data and saves it so users can share it digitally, with or without an internet connection. The term *files* can refer to a wide range of file types, as indicated by their filename extensions. They include documents (.doc, .pdf); presentations and videos (.ppt, .mp4, .mp3, .mov); and even 3D formats (.stl, .obj). In addition to these common file types, you can also include documents hosted and accessible online in this category, such as Google Slides presentations or PDFs saved to a Dropbox account.

In Figure 2.1, you will see some specific examples of how these different categories of content might be used at various grade levels. Of course, the possibilities are limitless.

Other Types of Content to Share with Students

• *Interactive panoramas:* for example, immersive 360-degree images

• *Applications:* for example, skill-practice apps, interactive simulations

• *Games:* for example, logic puzzles, multiplayer games

Physical spaces like large binders or overstuffed folders place limits on the tangible resources you can share with them. By contrast, digital spaces offer a seemingly endless amount of space to collect content for students as well as tech-friendly ways to organize and distribute resources to them. With these potentially unlimited online spaces, it's easy to get overwhelmed sorting through the options of content to share. It is important to be intentional with the resources you do decide to share with students and have a plan on how to get these supplemental resources into their hands. Let's explore what it means to select, organize, and distribute content—sometimes with the help of a chatbot—to meet the needs of all students.

FIGURE 2.1

Examples of Content to Share with Students

Type of Content	Grade Level			
	Early Elementary	Upper Elementary	Middle School	High School
Video	During a unit on fractions, students can watch an explanatory video from BrainPOP Jr.	While students learn about animal habitats, they can watch a video from National Geographic's YouTube channel.	Students can watch a clip posted by a local news organization to connect current events to a topic in a novel the class is reading.	As students learn about cultural diffusion, they can watch a TED-Ed video on "How corn conquered the world."
Text	Students can read a picture book on Epic (or use read-aloud support) connected to an upcoming holiday.	During a unit on the 13 colonies, students can read an encyclopedia entry from Britannica Kids.	While exploring issues around climate change, students can read a current events article on Newsela's website.	During a unit on economics, students can access a selection of articles from the *New York Times* and *USA Today*.
Audio	Students can listen to a folktale performed for the *Circle Round* podcast.	As they learn about informational text features, students can listen to an episode of the *Wow in the World* podcast.	During a unit on civic engagement, students can listen to an interview with a local councilperson.	Students can choose from a list of podcast episodes with interviews related to a content topic.
Images	Students can share observations as they look at images of an animal habitat.	Students can use domain-specific vocabulary to compare and contrast what they see when reviewing images of a landscape.	Students can review primary-source documents and share connections to what they have learned.	Students can review an image and ask questions to determine its authenticity.

(continued)

FIGURE 2.1 (*Continued*)

Examples of Content to Share with Students

Type of Content	Grade Level			
	Early Elementary	Upper Elementary	Middle School	High School
Graphics	Students can look at graphics that share information in sequence to connect with temporal words like *first, then, next,* and *finally.*	Students can discuss what type of symbols or visuals are used to complement the information that is shared.	Students can question the information presented in an infographic and make a list of follow-up questions to research.	Students can critique the design of an infographic and make suggestions for how it could be better organized.
Files	Students can review a slide-based presentation that includes images and simple text by swiping through each slide like a slideshow.	Students can read information presented in a Word document, changing the font size if needed.	Students can sort information presented in a spreadsheet in alphabetical order or from least to greatest.	Students can review multiple file types as they research a topic, including data in spreadsheets, information presented in a slide deck, or published work in a PDF.

Selecting Content

Selecting "just right" content for students requires consideration of several key factors: (1) learning goals, (2) background knowledge, (3) extension opportunities, and (4) student interest. Reviewing these four areas as you plan for an upcoming unit can help you decide what type of content will best suit your students' needs. Here are guiding questions for each area to use for your own planning or bring to a collaborative planning session with your colleagues:

Learning goals

- What do you want students to know and be able to do?
- What have you learned about students' needs from formative assessment data?
- How will you differentiate resources for small groups or individual students?

Background knowledge

- What will students need so they can make meaning of your course content?
- What differences in past experiences do your students have?
- What have your observations and conversations with students shown you?

Extension opportunities

- What areas may you not get a chance to cover in your traditional lessons?
- What cross-curricular connections would you like students to see?
- What content can students explore after a unit or lesson is finished?

Student interest

- What did students show an interest in during the unit or lesson?
- What additional video clips or podcast episodes would grab their attention?
- What subtopics can you gather resources on to help students dive deeper?

Ways to Gauge Student Interest

- Create and conduct an interest survey.
- Make time for a KWL (Know, Want to Know, Learned) chart, and review what students want to know about a topic.
- Hold informal discussions in which students share ideas they are curious about.
- Designate a "wonder wall" where students can post their lingering questions.

Handpicking content for students is nothing new. Differentiating instruction by selecting "just right" content is a well-recognized best practice and has nothing to do specifically with technology. Instead, digital tools, including those powered by AI, make it easier than ever to locate and distribute content that meets the needs of individual students.

As you select content, you can pay particular attention to tech-rich features that address students' needs. For example, you might find videos with closed-captioning options, share articles or ebooks with "read-to-me" features, or give students a choice of which podcast episode to listen to related to their interests as well as your content goals.

In Chapter 8, we will look more closely at formative assessment data and how this information will affect how you curate resources. Formative assessment should *inform* instruction, and it can help you select "just right" content for your classroom. Your pedagogical and content expertise should drive the decision about which content you select and share with students.

Using Chatbots to Curate Content

Chatbot technology can play a helpful role in curating content to share with students. You can use generative AI tools like ChatGPT or Gemini to gather resources for students. However, you need to know what you are looking for and why it would be helpful for students. It is also important to identify other conditions or descriptors of content before using a chatbot, such as length and age-appropriateness.

Educators can use prompts that request suggestions for videos, podcasts, and other recommendations for students. As we'll explore in the next chapter, generating a list of ideas is simply a starting point. You might find it is a more efficient way to search for supplemental methods than using a keyword search on Google or Pinterest. Searching for content with a chatbot isn't perfect, but it can speed up the search process and save you some time.

Once you have a vision of the types of resources you'd like to share with a group of students, you can open up a chatbot and ask for help. Here are a few prompts you can customize:

- Make a list of databases with [type of content] about [topic] for [grade level].

  Example: Make a list of databases with short videos about weather systems for 2nd graders.

- Recommend [genre] books about [topic] for [grade level].

  Example: Recommend historical fiction books about the California Gold Rush for 8th graders.

- Find [number] podcasts to share with [grade level] to help them learn about [topic].

  Example: Find five podcasts to share with high school juniors and seniors to help them learn about climate change.

To further customize these prompts, you might combine them with one of the following conditions:

- My students need [condition], so include resources with this in mind.

  Example: Make a list of databases with short videos about weather systems for 2nd graders. My students need captions, so include resources with this in mind.

- My students are interested in [topic], so include suggestions that connect in some way.

  Example: Recommend historical fiction books about the California Gold Rush for 8th graders. My students are interested in sports, so include suggestions that connect in some way.

- My students will access these resources on [device], so include resources they can use on this device.

  Example: Find five podcasts to share with high school juniors and seniors to help them learn about climate change. My students will access these resources on a smartphone, so include resources they can use on this device.

As you explore AI tools like chatbots, you might find they help you locate resources more efficiently than a traditional search engine. The specificity of the prompt you use will directly affect the results you receive. You may need to tweak the prompt a few times to get your desired result. It's up to you to craft a prompt that takes your students' needs into consideration; the chatbot won't know what your students need unless you include that information in the prompt you write.

Ways to Organize Your Chatbot Results

When giving a prompt to a chatbot, you can include your desired format in your prompt, such as "Make a table ..." or "Create a bulleted list. ..." Here is an example: "Create a table that lists popular kid-friendly songs about eating healthy. Include a column for date it was released, artist, song title, and length. Also add a column with one sentence explaining why you chose the song."

If you forget to add a format, the chatbot will choose one for you, such as a list or paragraph. However, you can follow up by asking the chatbot to place the results it gave you into a different format.

Organizing and Distributing Content

Selecting "just right" content for students is only the first step when curating materials to share. Digital tools can help you and your students organize that content so that it is easy to keep track of the resources you find. When organizing website links, video files, or whatever you would like to share with students, there are a few things to consider.

Many schools and districts use content or learning management systems (CMS or LMS), such as Google Classroom or Schoology, to organize and distribute resources. Many teachers already use tools such as Seesaw or Microsoft Teams in their classrooms to share content and assignments with students. Although I share ideas for organizing and distributing content in this chapter, I encourage you to first consider how you might share a link or file using the options already present in your workflow. Embrace the tools you currently have access to, and use the following options if you need additional support organizing and distributing content to students.

Organizing Resources Before You Share

What does the process of organizing resources for students look like in action? Organizing content is all about making it easy for you to know where "stuff" (files, links, and so on) is and how to get it in the hands of students.

In an early-elementary classroom, you might create three QR codes (with a tool like http://goqr.me), each connected to a different resource on an animal habitat. You can give students the option to choose which animal habitat to learn about by giving them three options for QR codes to scan. Alternatively, you might share a specific QR code with a particular group of students who you know will benefit from that particular content.

In an upper-elementary classroom, you might create a website for students studying severe storms using a website creation tool like Google Sites, Adobe Express, or Canva. The page you create can include links to a variety of YouTube clips related to different weather events. Students can watch each short clip and decide which type of storm they want to research for a collaborative class project.

In a middle school classroom, you might post links to four or five newspaper articles with profiles on different candidates running for local office. You might give students a choice on whom to read about, direct them to explore a particular article based on an interest they have expressed in the past, or share an article at an independent reading Lexile level for a student.

In a high school classroom, you might select three different narrative podcasts, each with a selection of episodes on a particular topic. After giving a quick intro to each choice, you might have students decide which series of episodes they would like to listen to as part of a research project.

Tips for Creating Collections

If you are organizing resources to share with students, you might decide to share just a few things at a time. Alternatively, you might have a larger amount of content for students to access—such as review materials at the end of a term—or you may want to create a collection of resources on a topic for you or your colleagues to access over a semester.

When it comes to managing resources, especially ones you want to share with students and colleagues, there are a few creation tools that make it easy to organize, curate, and share your favorites. Instead of bookmarking a bunch of pages or sending an email with links for students to click on, you can use a website-page builder (e.g., Microsoft Sway) or an interactive document (e.g., Google Docs) to create a collection of resources.

Although a CMS or LMS is always a great place to start, creating a public website or an interactive document is a great strategy if your students do not have access to a portal or a place to log in to access resources. You can create such a space using Wakelet, Google Sites, Microsoft Sway, Google Docs, or any other tool that lets you add a collection of links and share the page with a group of students. Once you create this page or document, you can continue to add links to resources you have curated for students.

Chatbots Can Help Organize Resources

In addition to locating resources, chatbots can help you organize a list of your resources. For example, you can paste a list of resources you want to share with students or colleagues into a chatbot along with one of the following prompts:

- Place these in alphabetical order . . .
- Put these videos in order from shortest to longest . . .
- Write a one-sentence summary for each of these resources . . .
- Give me a catchy title for this list of resources . . .

If you support educators in a classroom setting, you may take on the role of curator to help teachers locate resources to share with students. The ISTE Coaching Standards outline the importance of the role of coach as Collaborator, specifically Indicator 4.3.b, Identify Relevant Learning Content With Educators: "Partner with educators to identify digital learning content that is culturally relevant, developmentally appropriate and aligned to content standards."

Distributing Resources to Students (or Others)

As I mentioned earlier in this section, the way you distribute content might rely on systems you already use with students. This might include a space like Google Classroom, where you frequently post links for students, or a space like Wakelet, where you often create collections of links. Trying something new can be wonderful, but if your current system is working for you and your students, I encourage you to apply these organizational strategies within a space you already use to see if they can be adapted to a workflow or system you have in place.

Determining the right workflow for your class will depend on a few things. For example, what devices do students use, and are they able to log in to access content? If you know students are often on mobile devices like tablets or smartphones, you will want to make sure any links to videos or websites you send are mobile-friendly. If you know students do not have their own email addresses, you will want to make sure any links you list for them to click on—such as for a collection of current events articles—lead to a publicly accessible online space so they will not have to log in to a platform or website. A good practice is to try the workflow you are asking students to use before you share it with them, so you may want to test any links you share with them on the same type of device they will use to access content.

The intended audience for your collection might not be students, but colleagues teaching the same subject area, or families of students who would like to explore supplemental resources. Keep your audience in mind as you organize resources in a space that is easy to access and simple to navigate.

The ISTE Student Standards encourage children of all ages to see themselves as a Knowledge Constructor. Indicator 1.3.c, Curate Information, states, "Students curate information from digital resources using a variety of tools and methods to create collections of artifacts that demonstrate meaningful connections or conclusions."

Students as Curators

In addition to using digital tools to curate content yourself, you can bring students into the conversation around collecting and evaluating resources. When students take on the role of curators, they go beyond navigating digital spaces and shift to thinking deeply about different resources. The idea of students as curators adds another level of higher-order thinking skills to the activities we examined in Chapter 1.

In an early-elementary classroom, this approach could include having students watch you think aloud as you evaluate a resource before turning and talking with a partner about why a website is useful or not useful. In an upper-elementary, middle, or high school classroom, you might present a topic to students and have them create an annotated bibliography that includes a note on their evaluation of the usefulness of different resources.

Students who curate content must evaluate the quality, validity, and authority of different resources. They look for patterns and make decisions about which resources are the very best on a particular topic. This practice might go alongside a digital citizenship or media literacy curriculum, or you might integrate it into other subject areas.

Final Thoughts

Curation happens in classrooms every day. With or without digital tools, teachers choose the resources they know will help their students better understand a new concept. An essential use of EdTech is to locate and share resources in a variety of formats with the intention of supporting each student's individual needs. Just like a search engine, AI powered tools can help educators gather resources—but educators' expertise is needed to design prompts, review results, and ultimately decide what is the best fit for students.

Curation does not mean you need to search for 30 different math tutorial videos or 30 websites with 30 different science experiments. Instead, you can prioritize which content is best for your students, deciding who needs which resource at a particular time. Educators have a fundamental role in deciding what to share and when to share it with students. Thoughtful content curation can transform student learning experiences.

3

Generate Ideas and Resources with Artificial Intelligence

produce, craft, make, formulate, develop, forge

What would you do with more hours in the school week? Perhaps you would have more time to create engaging lessons for students, to design differentiated learning experiences, or to simply take a deep breath after a long day. The action word in this chapter's title is **generate** because our emphasis in this section of the book is on what educators can make with generative artificial intelligence tools. We'll particularly focus on using these tools to save you time that you can reallocate throughout the school week. As much as I would like to quantify this time and claim that you will save 10 hours a week with the help of AI tools, that feels inauthentic to my general principle that technology is what you make of it.

Generative AI is here to stay—and it is playing a part in how we accomplish everyday tasks. A chatbot like ChatGPT or Claude can give advice on what to do with 20 pounds of apples after a day of apple picking (I've tried that) or help you plan an itinerary for an upcoming trip (I've tried that, too), but it's only as good as the prompt it's given. To fully leverage the power and possibilities of artificial intelligence, you need to know what's possible. This chapter is about using generative AI to help you accomplish big and small tasks throughout the school week.

Why Is This Essential?

In a world where AI is playing an ever-increasing role, it is critical that educators understand how to use AI-powered tools in their practice alongside the potential implications for the future of this field. The recent report "Artificial Intelligence and the Future of Teaching and Learning" stresses the importance of having "humans in the loop" when using AI in education settings, offering the comparison of "an electric bike, [where] the human is fully aware and fully in control, but their burden is less, and their effort is multiplied by a complementary technological enhancement" (U.S. Department of Education, Office of Educational Technology, 2023, p. 53).

Many teachers have explored generative AI tools like ChatGPT: a 2023 study from the Walton Family Foundation found that "[w]ithin two months of its introduction, a 51% majority of teachers reported using ChatGPT, with 40% using it at least once a week" (para. 3). It is essential that educators understand how this technology can impact their instructional planning and everyday interactions with technology. Educators in all roles can use generative AI to help them accomplish several goals, including building a foundational understanding of generative AI and its implications for the wider world, accelerating their workflow by streamlining tasks, and generating engaging instructional resources for students.

Common Chatbot Terms

- *Prompt:* a message or question that tells a chatbot what action to take

- *Input:* the task, question, or set of instructions (typically in the form of a prompt) that tells AI what to do

- *Output:* the content produced by generative AI, like a table or paragraph created by a chatbot

- *Prompt engineering:* the skill of writing and refining questions, tasks, or instructions for generative AI tools to help achieve the desired result

---

It is crucial that educators begin to consider the power and influence of generative AI. The ISTE Education Leaders Standard 3.5, Connected Learner, emphasizes the importance of understanding what is new in educational technology. Standard Indicator 3.5.a, Stay Current on Innovation in Learning, states, "Set goals to remain current on emerging technologies for learning, innovations in pedagogy and advancements in the learning sciences."

What Is Generative AI?

Artificial intelligence encompasses a variety of technology, from a streaming service that anticipates what you might want to watch to a messaging tool that predicts words to fill in next as you text a friend or family member. AI performs tasks that normally only people can do, like respond to questions, solve problems, and make decisions—it imitates a human.

Generative AI *generates,* or creates, content. This content can include images, videos, music, and text. Instead of searching for pre-existing content like using a search engine, generative AI creates content by combining information from a variety of sources. In this chapter, and throughout *EdTech Essentials,* we'll focus primarily on chatbots like ChatGPT, which has gained popularity across education spaces and various industries since its public release in late 2022. We'll also examine the possibilities for generating images with AI, which requires a similar prompt-engineering skill.

Using Chatbots to Generate Ideas and Resources

One of the most popular ways to use generative AI is to create a text output using a chatbot. A chatbot answers questions and provides information based on your submitted instructions, queries, or prompts. It is a tool that requires users to know what questions to ask to get the desired output. Unlike a search engine that provides a list of resources related to a topic, a chatbot generates responses to questions or prompts that are more fully formed and mimic the way a human would respond to a query or task.

Whether you are a classroom teacher or help the educators in your school with curriculum planning, a chatbot can support your work on various fronts. It can help you brainstorm a direction for your next lesson, develop activities for different groups of students, and generate ideas to plan an upcoming unit of study. But you must ask it to help you

---

ChatGPT and More

ChatGPT is a chatbot developed by OpenAI that launched in the fall of 2022. *GPT* stands for *generative pre-trained transformers,* which is a family of language models that uses text created by humans to help it learn how to provide a human-like response to a query. For now, there is a free version and a premium paid version called ChatGPT Plus that produces responses a bit more quickly and provides additional features, such as plugins that connect the technology in ChatGPT to other tools. I am confident that you can accomplish great things with the free versions of ChatGPT and other generative AI technology tools, and that is where I would encourage you to start.

ChatGPT is not the only type of generative AI technology, and you may want to explore the list below:

- ChatGPT (OpenAI): https://chat.openai.com
- Claude (Anthropic): https://claude.ai
- Gemini (Google): https://gemini.google.com

accomplish your goals with a specific prompt that takes into consideration the unique factors of your learning environment.

When using a chatbot to generate ideas, you can start with a *simple* prompt and add in additional considerations or follow-up questions to help you achieve the desired output. Let's look at a few areas where using a chatbot can save you time working toward goals: student engagement, assessment, and differentiation.

Student Engagement

If your students seem distant or uninterested in the topic you are teaching, you can use a chatbot to generate activity ideas related to their interests. This is an opportunity to find cross-curricular applications and connections to high-interest topics that you can leverage to boost student engagement, as shown in the following sample prompts:

- I'm teaching [topic] to [grade level] and they love [interests]. Make a list of connections that can help them stay engaged and retain knowledge.
- I want to infuse literacy skills into a new unit on [topic] for a group of [grade level] students. Give me a list of [adjective] ideas to help students strengthen [literacy skill].
- Make a list of 10 unexpected ways to introduce [topic] to [grade level] students.

Note: Instead of (or in addition to) including the grade level of your students, you can add a description such as "students in an after-school program ranging from ages 9 to 12" or "students who are learning English as a new language."

Assessment

The work of crafting assignments and designing assessments for students is an important part of an educator's role. A chatbot can support your assessment routines by helping you design activities that check for understanding. The following are examples of prompts you might try:

- Make a list of [number] writing prompts I can share with students in [grade level] to have them write about [topic].
- My students are [task] and expected to [expectation]. I want to give them feedback on [objective] related to [standard]. What kinds of things can I say to them to help them [goal]?

Easy EdTech Podcast: 248

Differentiation

Most educators would agree that differentiated instruction is an important part of reaching all students—*and* that this process takes valuable planning time. Generative AI can help speed this process and create customized resources to support your differentiation goal. The following sample prompts show how you might use this tool in such a way:

- Break down [topic] into smaller, easier-to-understand parts. Use analogies and real-life examples to simplify the concept and make it more relatable to [grade level].
- Explain the process of [task] in [number] steps for [grade level]. Keep in mind that [condition].
- Make a list of important vocabulary words related to [topic] for [grade level].
- Find [number] podcasts to share with [grade level] to help them learn about [topic].

Throughout this book, the term *differentiation* appears alongside suggestions and strategies for developing learning experiences that are "just right" for individual students. ISTE Educator Standard Indicator 2.5.a, Accommodate Learner Differences, states, "Use technology to create, adapt and personalize learning experiences that foster independent learning and accommodate learner differences and needs." Generative AI can help educators create differentiated resources for their students.

Generating Images with AI

Image generation tools take a spin on the ways to use AI previously described. Instead of taking a text input and providing a text output in a format like a list, paragraph, or table, these tools can take a text input and provide an image as the output. Like the prompt engineering described earlier in this chapter, a user must create a prompt that describes what they are looking to create. For example, if you are preparing a creative writing activity related to wintertime, you might use the prompt "A penguin with a suitcase holding a map on an iceberg" to generate your image.

Although there isn't a set formula for creating a prompt, there are a few things to take into consideration. In most instances, you will want to include a subject, a setting, an action, and a mood in your prompt. You can also indicate whether you want the output to feel more photorealistic or more cartoonish. Some tools have filters that allow you to turn on and off certain constraints, including color palette and image sizing.

Customize Your Prompts

To make your prompts more specific, add a condition that provides additional information. Try adding information on one of the following areas to make your prompt more specific:

- Learning objective or curriculum goal
- Standard or cross-curricular connection
- Grade level or description of student needs
- Student interest or overview of past experiences

Reasons to Use AI Images

In a classroom setting, you may find that using an image generation tool saves you time from conducting searches on Google Images for pictures that may or may not include permission for sharing. It can help you explain a concept with illustrations and refresh existing instructional materials so content is of higher interest to your students.

Replace a search. If you've spent precious planning time searching for an image to add to a presentation for students, you might consider replacing the search by generating your own image. When you know what you're looking for, you can type in a prompt to find a "just right" image to share with students. A Google Images search often provides results that you do not have permission to reuse or modify. This factor may be an important part of your choice to use an AI-powered image generation tool.

Upgrade old resources. When I was a classroom teacher, there were years when I taught the same unit as the previous year. Creating customized images is a great way to upgrade old resources that need a refresh. For example, if you are teaching a unit on landforms and your students love dogs, you might generate an image using the prompt "A yellow Labrador retriever standing on a plateau wearing a backpack on a sunny day." You can use these types of tools to boost students' engagement and help them retain information.

Explain complex ideas. Images can help illustrate complex topics, particularly if you break them down into parts and want a corresponding image for each step. If you are breaking down a concept into parts, such as explaining different geometric shapes or a process like photosynthesis, you might find that images can help students grasp each section.

One of my favorite ways to introduce the possibilities—and complexities—of generative AI tools is with a "guess the prompt" activity. In webinars and in-person workshops, I've tried this with hundreds (maybe thousands) of educators, and you might try it with students or colleagues if you are talking about prompt generation, too. For this activity, go to an image generation tool and type in a prompt to generate an image. You are welcome to borrow one of my favorites: "a polar bear dancing in New York City at nighttime." Download the image, then show the image to your group. Ask them to talk with a partner about what type of prompt could generate this image, then ask them to share with the whole group. When I do this, I like to use the "open-ended question" feature in Mentimeter. After you reveal the results, you can ask the group to share some things they might add to the prompt, or something that surprised them about the input and output.

Tools for Creating Images

There are a handful of tools that allow you to create images using a text prompt, including the following:

- Adobe Firefly (accessible on its own or in Adobe Express)
- Canva's Magic Media app
- DALL-E from OpenAI

Working Smarter, Not Harder

The phrase "working smarter, not harder" may feel overused, but it has been a guiding light in my conversations with educators on the power of generative AI. In workshops and webinars, I often ask the question "What is taking you too much time?" In addition to the generation of ideas and resources described in this chapter, this question could also encompass the tedious or administrative tasks that are part of your everyday work. For the past decade, I have focused on making EdTech easier for educators by sharing tips and strategies to support technology integration and boost productivity. Generative AI tools have made it easier than ever to save time throughout the school week.

Let's look at a few areas where you may feel swamped and explore prompts you can tailor to the chatbot of your choice to help lighten your workload.

Email Correspondence

A chatbot can help you get a jump start on crafting emails by drafting a template you can customize and then reuse throughout the school year.

You can also use a chatbot to revise emails that you have already written but need improvement. Here are two sample prompts:

- Write a message to welcome new families to our school. Include our mission of [insert mission], and a reminder to [insert reminder].
- Create a template for an email that reminds families about an upcoming field trip. Include a bulleted list with space for me to add in the specifics (e.g., time, place, things to bring).

Creating Review Materials

When sharing resources with students, such as review materials, you may want additional support in locating supplemental resources. A chatbot can help with this task, as shown in the following prompts:

- Use bold, italic, and underlining to highlight key information and draw attention to important points.
- Suggest a visual that will help students retain information about each key point in this outline.
- Make a playlist of videos that are under [number] minutes long to help students in my [grade level] class learn about [skill].

Organizing Information

A chatbot can help speed up time-consuming tasks—things you could clearly do yourself but might not be the best use of your time. For the following examples, you may already have a piece of text that you include alongside your prompt; just be sure to remove any personal, private, or sensitive information.

- Turn this list into a table with one column for [category] and another column for [category].
- Add headings and subheadings to this text [paste text].
- Make me a spreadsheet for tracking my daily habits with columns for [date], [habit #1], [habit #2], and [habit #3].
- Summarize my notes from this meeting [paste text].

Going Further with AI

In this chapter, we've looked at generative AI—specifically, chatbots that respond to text input and provide text or image output. The prompts on the previous pages (and on the following pages, too) are designed for use with chatbots like ChatGPT, Claude, or Gemini. As you continue to explore AI and its impact on education, the following are a handful of education-specific tools and "next-level" prompts to try out.

Examine Education-Specific Tools

Easy EdTech Podcast: 241

In an episode of my (2023a) *Easy EdTech Podcast,* I shared "4 Types of AI Tools Every Teacher Should Know About" (to listen, scan the QR code). The types of tools I covered included chatbots and image creators, described earlier in this chapter, as well as question generators and presentation creators. Let's examine what is possible when educators use tools in the last two categories.

Question generators. These tools take information such as topic, objective, standard, and grade level and create a series of questions you can share with students to check for understanding. This type of tool saves you time creating multiple-choice questions, open-ended questions, and a variety of other question types. When using a question generator, you will want to review the information for accuracy and add or remove questions as needed to make sure they are the right fit for your group. In this category of tools, you might try Conker to generate a mix of questions or Pressto's Writing Assistant to suggest prompts alongside important vocabulary words.

Presentation creators. These tools can help you create presentation slide decks to share with students, speeding up the design process, helping you find supporting media, and even adding in interactive activities. Similar to the output from question generators, you will need to use your expert eye to make sure they are the right fit for your group. In this category, you might try Curipod to make interactive presentations or use Canva's Magic Media text-to-image tool.

Try "Next-Level" Prompts

If you have experience engineering prompts, you may be ready to add conditions that take a simple prompt to the next level. Here are a few suggestions of what you might add to a prompt you have written to get a stronger output:

- Give me multiple options to choose from.
- Here is an example of the type of result I'm looking for [insert example].

- I don't want a result like [insert example] or [insert example].
- Ask me questions I can respond to, so you can give me a better result.

Share Your Learning

As you continue to spend time with the EdTech essential *generate*, you are in a fantastic position to share your learning. This is an evolving space, so even if you shy away from using the term *expert* to describe what you have accomplished using chatbots, you may be the expert in your school community. To share your learning and support your colleagues, you can create a collection of prompts that have worked well for you and connect to a shared need at your school. You might also decide to host a lunch-and-learn to let your colleagues know what is possible with AI and how it is saving you time this school year. Finally, if you write a weekly or monthly newsletter to your colleagues, consider including a favorite prompt at the bottom of the newsletter or a suggested AI tool to explore.

Final Thoughts

You may already use technology to support your instructional planning. From a Google search for "lesson ideas on ecosystems" to a Pinterest exploration of "graphic organizers for a cause-and-effect lesson," there are numerous popular online spaces to go to for planning and inspiration. In the same way one of these spaces can help you gather ideas or jump-start your planning process, a chatbot can deliver responses to questions that offer ideas and inspiration, too.

When I talk to educators about the use of generative AI for instructional planning and administrative tasks, I often say that this technology helps get us 80 percent of the way there. This is an estimate, of course, but my goal is to illustrate that generative AI can save us lots of time when we use it strategically—but it will not replace our judgment and expertise. We will still need to customize responses to meet our goals and decide what to use and what to discard as we review the output from our query. Chatbot responses are not perfect and, as we'll explore in the next chapter, you'll want to review digital content created with AI to make sure it is worthy of sharing.

Updated AI Resources

AI in education is continually evolving, including the release of new tools that leverage AI. To stay up-to-date with changes in this space, the following links (also accessible via the QR codes) will take you to a handful of my resources:

- AI blog posts: https://classtechtips.com/tag/ai-blog-post

AI Blog
Posts

- AI podcast episodes: https://classtechtips.com/tag/ai-podcast

AI Podcast
Episodes

- Weekly newsletter: https://classtechtips.com/newsletter

Weekly
Newsletter

4

Evaluate Digital Content
with an AI Mindset

connect, review, examine, gauge, judge, inspect

Evaluating sources is a crucial component of successfully navigating an online space—especially in a world where online content could have been generated with artificial intelligence. In the first edition of this book, I included a section on evaluating sources in Chapter 1 (Navigating Online Spaces Effectively). For this edition, I moved that section to this new chapter, in which we'll explore the essential **evaluate** through three lenses, including (1) examining content generated by AI, (2) emphasizing process in student learning artifacts, and (3) integrating digital citizenship skills into our conversation on AI. It is essential to have a strong foundation for evaluating sources as students navigate digital spaces and educators curate content to share with them. As content generated with AI becomes increasingly prevalent, understanding this concept is more important than ever.

Why Is This Essential?

The ability to sort through content and gauge authenticity and authority is an indispensable skill for students of all ages. Students should be able to determine where information is coming from and whether the source they have found is trustworthy. Doing so is an important aspect of digital citizenship—a topic that appears throughout this book.

For educators exploring the power of AI, an understanding of the limitations of using AI to generate content and a need to evaluate content created or suggested by a generative AI tool is also critical. In "Assigning AI: Seven Approaches for Students, with Prompts," Mollick and Mollick (2023) explore the potential of AI tools, including the use of "AI as teammate," and describe the power and risks associated with using chatbots to promote collaboration and offer support. Mollick and Mollick warn that "AI can confabulate or make up facts. . . . It can give teams advice that isn't specific or contextualized" (p. 30). This is one of the risks of using AI ourselves or interacting with AI-generated content.

Education leaders have an important role to play in modeling how to evaluate content. ISTE Education Leader Standard Indicator 4.7.c, Foster Media Evaluation, addresses this aspect of a leader's role, stating that leaders should "Support educators and students in critically examining online media sources and identifying underlying assumptions." In a world where generative AI can create content that is hard to distinguish from the "real thing," this is particularly notable.

Examining Digital Content

The reality that not all digital content is labeled as "created with AI" can further complicate the task of determining whether content is accurate and reliable and reinforces the importance of evaluating the content—text, audio, video, and images—we come across in digital spaces. As consumers of a wide range of digital content, we need to expand our view of what it means to examine and evaluate content for authority, accuracy, and authenticity.

Authority

When looking at resources in print or digital format, students must determine if a source is legitimate and whether the author or creator is well versed enough to share information on a topic. Essentially, students must ask, "Is this a trusted source?" In the early days of navigating online spaces, we would often first look at the domain of a website to evaluate its authority—for example, .edu, .org, or .com. Although students can still consider this information when evaluating a source, it is only part of the equation. The background and bias of the author and organization should also be a consideration.

Here are a few questions you can use when modeling for students how to evaluate a source. Students can also use these questions when working independently.

- Who wrote this? Who produced this? Who recorded this?
- Who is the owner of this website? Who made this video or podcast recording?
- Is this author or organization qualified to share this information?
- Does this author or organization have any clear bias?
- Is this content sponsored by another company?
- This audio/video clip doesn't seem quite right; where can I go to confirm its authenticity?
- Does the author cite sources for any information referenced or claims made?

When searching online with students, you can model your own thinking when coming across a new source. Again, students should hear you thinking aloud, deciding when to use a resource and when to move on and look for something new. This can happen during teachable or unplanned moments as well as during searches you intentionally model for students.

Accuracy

In the previous chapter, we discussed strategies for generating content using AI tools and touched on the importance of checking the accuracy of the output. Examining a source for accuracy isn't just essential for interacting with AI but also an important part of reviewing print or digital content. Similar to the preceding list of questions related to authority, you might model for students how you check information by looking at two sources. For example, you might use a sentence starter like one of the following as you model how to fact-check information you've read, viewed, or heard in a digital space:

- This doesn't look quite right; let's check another source . . .
- I want to make sure I have accurate information; I wonder where else I can look . . .
- Before using this information, I want to confirm it's correct . . .

If content is generated with AI, it might include an attribution alongside it, but this type of disclosure is not guaranteed or widely regulated at this time.

Authenticity

To determine whether a piece of content is authentic, it's important to understand what generative AI can actually create. Although there are many ways to use AI, in this book we have primarily explored text and image output and the way in which an educator might use these types of media to create content to share with students, colleagues, and families. As consumers, you and your students will come across a variety of creations generated with AI tools as you navigate online spaces. These experiences can spark important conversations on the authenticity of a piece of text, an image, a video, or an audio file.

When it comes to evaluating the authenticity of text, you may use some of the same review questions previously listed to verify its authority and accuracy. For image, video, and audio content—particularly content related to current events or divisive political issues—determining authenticity may feel like a larger struggle.

You may be familiar with the term *deepfake* or have encountered media that just didn't seem "right." In an article for the *New York Times*, Satariano and Mozur (2023) describe what you might see when viewing AI-generated video content: "Something was off. Their voices were stilted and failed to sync with the movement of their mouths. Their faces had a pixelated, video-game quality and their hair appeared unnaturally plastered to the head. The captions were filled with grammatical mistakes" (para. 3). Although something might seem "off" when interacting with AI-generated content in its current form, this technology is only getting stronger—making it increasingly difficult to determine whether an image, a video, or an audio recording is indeed authentic. Keeping this in mind as you curate content is an essential part of your role as an evaluator. You may also decide to review examples of AI-generated multimedia with students to model how you question the authenticity of an image, video, or audio recording that is shared with you or you encounter online.

To model this skill, you might use sentence starters like the following:

- The sound doesn't match up to the video very well; I wonder if . . .
- This picture seems hard to believe. Where can I verify its authenticity . . . ?
- This audio recording feels "off," and I can't put my finger on why. Let's double-check with . . .

The ability of AI-generated content to simulate a person's voice or movement to create inauthentic images of people, places, and current events is certainly alarming. As an educator, you might decide to connect conversations on media literacy to English language arts (ELA) skills like close reading or a social studies topic like the use of propaganda during different moments in history.

Emphasizing Process in Student Learning Artifacts

One concern I have heard from educators in my conversations about AI, specifically generative AI, is how to stop students from using these tools to complete their work. In the past, we may have had similar conversations in education on the use of a calculator (now easily accessible on our mobile phones) or search engines like Google (which are now part of our everyday lives). I mention these examples not to dismiss the valid concerns you or your colleagues might hold, but to reframe the conversation on evaluating student work to place more emphasis on celebrating the process students go through when creating learning artifacts.

In the next chapter, we'll look at student creation examples and discuss what these can look like in a classroom setting. But first, let's set a foundation for how to address concerns about how generative AI might affect student learning artifacts and how you can intentionally design learning experiences with this in mind. The following are three ways you might pause to celebrate students and evaluate their progress:

- **Brainstorming.** Encourage students to spend time brainstorming ideas before moving in one direction for a project. This could include sketchnoting or using a digital whiteboard tool that allows students to connect ideas or build upon a series of ideas. Celebrate this artifact of learning by having students share their top three ideas with classmates.
- **Drafting with feedback.** Build time within the learning process to have students solicit and receive feedback on their work. This is an important collaborative action that we'll examine later in this book alongside strategies for collaborating in digital spaces. Incorporating feedback into the creative process holds students accountable for the first steps in bringing an idea to life.

- **Publishing with notes.** In my role as a classroom teacher, I would ask students to include their graphic organizers and drafts in a packet with their final piece of writing before displaying it on our hallway bulletin board or adding it to their portfolio. Before the word *ChatGPT* entered our collective lexicon, I knew it was important to celebrate the process in addition to the product. You might ask students to publish their work with notes on the process, such as a complementary audio recording that discusses the decisions they made during the creative process.

Leveraging Originality Reports

Many schools and districts use software to detect plagiarism, particularly at the secondary level. This practice began before the widespread use of generative AI tools like ChatGPT. In the age of AI, it may feel tempting to rely on these tools to evaluate student work, but it can be hard to pinpoint how and whether content was generated with the help of an AI tool. If you are using originality reports, leading with an accusation can damage relationships and hinder future conversations about the role of AI for teaching and learning. Instead, you may want to refer to any discrepancies in an originality report more as a way to spark conversations about digital citizenship and the process of students' creations than for any punitive measures.

Having "eyes on the process" can reinforce the concept that student creations are evolving and include multiple iterations, and the final component is just one piece of the learning journey to celebrate. Although your students may incorporate AI tools into their work now or in the future—with or without your endorsement or approval—building a routine that includes a celebration of the student learning process can better prepare them for the expectation that their own work is accurate and authentic.

Practicing Digital Citizenship

Evaluation is an essential skill in both online and offline learning experiences. It is a higher-level cognitive process included in the revised Bloom's taxonomy (Anderson & Krathwohl, 2001) and an important part of our conversation on navigating online spaces effectively, particularly in the age of AI. Your students might take part in a formal digital citizenship curriculum, or their experiences with digital citizenship may be less structured. Activities that include evaluating sources reinforce this effort and enable students to apply what they have learned, but they are only part of the puzzle.

You might decide to connect a conversation on a student's contribution to digital spaces to discussions on the use of AI-generated content. In addition to evaluating content online for authority, accuracy, and authenticity, students can evaluate their own choices as they participate in digital spaces, including the impact of sharing AI-generated content without proper attribution.

The ISTE Student Standards include 1.2, Digital Citizen. Indicator 1.2.a, Digital Footprint, states, "Students cultivate and manage their digital identity and reputation, and are aware of the permanence of their actions in the digital world," and Indicator 1.2.c, Intellectual Property, states, "Students demonstrate an understanding of and respect for the rights and obligations of using and sharing intellectual property."

We've discussed the importance of celebrating the process and journey of student creators to encourage them to see AI as a tool, not a quick fix for writing an essay or answering homework questions. You may decide to incorporate a conversation about students' role as digital citizens, including an emphasis on their digital footprint and use of intellectual property. For example, you might lead a lesson that asks students to list the adjectives they would like someone to use to describe them, and students can brainstorm how their actions online (i.e., their digital footprint) should look if they want to live up to that description. Appendix E includes some resources for consideration that support your teaching around digital citizenship.

Final Thoughts

In a world where AI-generated content may appear on our laptops, tablets, and smartphones, it is important for educators and students to understand the importance of evaluating digital content. As consumers, we can examine content generated by AI and model for students how to approach a piece of media with skepticism until we are confident in its authority, accuracy, and authenticity. To support student creators, we can place an emphasis on process in the creation and evaluation of learning artifacts and integrate digital citizenship skills into our conversations about AI. In the next few chapters, we'll continue to explore the impact of artificial intelligence on teaching and learning, including the ways in which we help students explore the world.

5

Explore the World with Students

investigate, inquire, examine, look into, research, inspect, study, search

If you have ever taken students on a field trip, played a video clip featuring a new corner of the world, or had a guest speaker visit your class (in person or virtually), you know the power of sharing new experiences with students to help them better understand the world around them. In addition to organizing these types of activities for students, we want to help students build the capacity to explore their world with digital tools.

We can use online spaces to **explore** the world in different ways. Some of us go on deep dives via a search engine, with one starter question leading to many more. Others type a question or prompt into a chatbot and are delighted to find the answer. In Chapter 1, we looked at the importance of helping students effectively navigate online spaces. In this chapter, we will move beyond navigation to think about how to use online tools to explore the world. We will examine the connection between using technology to explore different places and the role it plays in building empathy, piquing student curiosity, and helping students think critically and deeply about people, places, and things.

Why Is This Essential?

Providing opportunities for students to explore the world can boost student interest and engagement. In an overview of research on curiosity in the classroom for *The Atlantic,* Scott Barry Kaufman (2017) asserts that "the power of curiosity to contribute not only to high achievement, but also to a fulfilling existence, cannot be emphasized enough" (para. 2) and describes stimulating classroom activities as "those that offer . . . novelty, surprise, and complexity, allowing greater autonomy and student choice [and encouraging] students to ask questions [and] question assumptions" (para. 17).

When students use digital tools to explore the world, they can go beyond simply learning facts about a new place. Virtual exploration helps them gain a better understanding of others through their culture, geography, and unique experiences. Although traveling the world and talking to new people in face-to-face interactions is ideal, online experiences can strengthen connections and help students learn about the lives of others whom they may never encounter in the town or city where they live.

If you are familiar with ASCD's Whole Child Initiative, you may have examined the indicators that go along with each of the basic principles related to educating the whole child. The tenet "Engaged" includes an indicator for placing students' learning in a context that helps them explore and better understand their world. This indicator states: "Our teachers use a range of inquiry-based, experiential learning tasks and activities to help all students deepen their understanding of what they are learning and why they are learning it" (ASCD, n.d.).

The ISTE Student Standards also stress the importance of helping students become global collaborators. Indicator 1.7.d states, "Students explore local and global issues and use collaborative technologies to work with others to investigate solutions."

When used intentionally, education technology gives students more ways to learn about the world around them, increase their connections, and research issues facing their own community and communities far away.

Exploring the World to Better Understand It

Having students read about a new place in a textbook is not sufficient if we are truly committed to helping them better understand the world around them. When used strategically, digital tools can provide immersive experiences for students. These experiences can present new information, honor students' questions, spark their curiosity, and help them establish a more well-rounded picture of the lives and experiences of people who might not live the way they do.

In Chapter 1, we noted, "We don't know what we don't know." This observation is true for learners of all ages, and you have probably experienced plenty of your own learning moments that fall into this category. More than just introducing students to new ideas, people, and places, it is essential that we build their capacity for understanding how to explore the world. This goal is easier than ever to accomplish with technology's capability of giving students access to new places.

Building Empathy

Empathy is the ability to understand the experiences and perspectives of others by placing yourself in someone else's shoes to see a situation from their viewpoint. To empathize with someone, students need to better understand what life is like in other parts of the world, hear the voices of people with life experiences that vary from their own, and know where to go to learn more about someone's backgrounds and perspectives.

Where does technology come into play? Digital tools help students access information, build connections, and chronicle their growth through reflections. All these practices help students learn about something new with a stated intention. Let's explore some of the ways you can leverage technology to help students build empathy throughout the school year.

Access. Students can learn about another person's life in many different ways. They might listen to a podcast episode in which a person shares their perspective on a current events issue, read an interview in an online magazine, or watch a video in which someone responds to a question. Students now have seemingly endless access to the ideas and perspectives of people in different parts of the world.

The passive experiences of listening, reading, or watching multimedia content can provide immense value as students learn about the life of someone else. You may curate these experiences for students (see Chapter 2) or provide suggestions about where students can go to conduct research and learn more about a person, place, or issue. You might create a collection of online resources using a tool like Wakelet to organize links students can explore to learn more about a part of the world. Alternatively, you might create a playlist of videos on YouTube, including interviews with experts on a topic from across the globe.

For example, if you are teaching a lesson on biodiversity to middle school students, you might locate interviews with people who live in a community near the Amazon rainforest and can speak about the ways deforestation has affected their lives. The interviews can supplement the conversations you have with students about the impact on the animals and plants in that ecosystem by providing the perspective of someone's lived experience.

Connections. In addition to helping students access information for more passive learning experiences, we now have an ability like never before to connect students *directly* with people who can speak about their personal experiences. The idea of fostering connections with other people is not novel or unique to tech-friendly environments—just think back to any pen pal experiences from your past—but the added value technology brings is manifold. Technology can make these connections happen with ease and efficiency, allow students to view supporting resources hosted online, and provide the opportunity to scale these learning experiences in both depth and frequency.

Connections related to empathy building provide space for conversations, questions, and listening. They may happen in a synchronous environment, in which two groups log in at the same time to participate in live conversation, or they may happen asynchronously. There are benefits to both options: an asynchronous exchange is logistically simpler, whereas a live meeting brings a higher level of excitement.

In an asynchronous environment, one group might post a question or share a response, and the other group can check in and follow up with a question or response of its own. For example,

Turning Empathy into Action

In *Teach Boldly: Using EdTech for Social Good,* ISTE author Jennifer Williams (2019) describes how to take a commitment to empathy building and turn it into action: "By using EdTech for social good, we can collectively drive change. Work in this area can take many forms: students creating campaigns, advocating for causes, or taking dedicated actions as activists for change" (p. 7).

Tools for Interactive Journaling

Interactive journaling is a practice you might explore with students. They could participate in a regular journaling practice where they provide a new entry once or twice a week. When searching for an interactive tool, look for the following features:

- The ability to add a voice recording to a page
- Simple video recording
- Voice-to-text dictation

imagine you are working with a group of 1st graders in Delaware who are learning about popular food dishes from around the world. They might connect with a school in Japan and post questions about what students eat for lunch and share what they eat at school every day. Although the students in Japan are in another time zone—eating lunch when the students in Delaware are fast asleep—they can post their answers so the students in Delaware can check in with them the next day. Later in this chapter, we will further explore videoconferencing and strategies for facilitating these types of conversations.

Reflections. Building empathy might be your primary goal while working with students to explore the world with digital tools. Although these experiences may be meaningful in the moment, encouraging students to reflect and think about their new learnings can make the impact long-lasting. When you include time for reflection, students can take a step back to pause and perhaps chronicle their growth in a journal entry to capture their feelings about an experience. A reflective journaling activity could use a digital format, with students recording a video or audio response to describe their experience. You might use prompts such as these:

- What surprised you about this interaction?
- What do you want to learn more about?
- Who else can give you a perspective on this issue?
- Did this conversation confirm or challenge your thinking about this topic?

The Role of SEL

As students use EdTech to explore the world, you might decide to make connections to social and emotional learning (SEL) goals. If you are new to SEL, here is how the Collaborative for Academic, Social, and Emotional Learning (CASEL, n.d.) defines the term:

The process through which all young people and adults acquire and apply the knowledge, skills, and attitudes to develop healthy identities, manage emotions and achieve personal and collective goals, feel and show empathy for others, establish and maintain supportive relationships, and make responsible and caring decisions.

CASEL's framework comprises five core competencies: self-awareness, self-management, social awareness, relationship skills, and responsible decision making. Education technology experiences around exploration will not automatically transfer to building SEL skills. However, SEL goals may determine the direction certain activities take or may be worth noting when you are planning online interactions for students.

For example, in an elementary classroom, students might read a piece of realistic fiction together as a class and then explore the setting of the book by "walking" around an interactive panorama of the place referenced in the book using a resource found on the Google Arts & Culture platform. In a middle school classroom, students might use graphic organizers in Book Creator to create an interactive Venn diagram illustrating ways their lives are similar to or different from those of people in another part of the world. They can add links, voice notes, and other features to make their graphic organizers interactive. In a high school classroom, students might develop questions to ask a group of students in a country a few time zones away. They could conduct a videoconference through Zoom or Google Meet to ask their distant counterparts about their experience applying to a university or their goals for future careers.

> **Teachable Moments**
>
> When a new place or location unexpectedly becomes part of a conversation, pause to give students a moment (e.g., 60 seconds) to explore some aspect of it. Here are a few prompts you can use:
>
> - How far is this place from where we live? Let's put it into Google Maps and see.
> - What are some little-known facts about this place? Let's put our question into a chatbot like ChatGPT.
> - What is the weather like there? Let's search on Weather.com.
> - What time zone are they in? Let's do a web search.
> - Do they speak more than one language there? Let's do a voice search and ask Siri or Alexa.
> - What does this place have in common with where we live? Let's craft a prompt to add to a chatbot like Gemini.

VR and AR: Exploring the World with Emerging Technologies

The term *emerging technologies* refers to technologies that have not quite reached their full potential or widespread adoption. Prime examples are virtual reality (VR) and augmented reality (AR). VR and AR tools have been around for quite some time, and you may already have tried out one or both, but the adoption rate, including classroom use, is not widespread. Although you might see these technologies in some schools, they are not ubiquitous.

What is the added value of emerging technologies in a classroom setting? The answer really depends on the type of technology you are referring to and the use you have in mind. The benefits to students (or anyone) will vary depending on how you use them. Determining your intention for introducing new technology into your learning environment is key.

Among the many ways for students to explore the world, virtual reality and augmented reality are high on the list. These types of technology can help students learn about new places and the lives of people in different corners of the world. They can act as a vehicle to "transport" students to a new space, to see the scale of a place they have never visited, to make connections with content from other sources, and to spark their curiosity for further inquiry.

Augmented reality and virtual reality can accomplish some of the same goals of more commonly used technologies, but there are notable differences in their potential uses. Augmented reality layers a digital experience on top of a real-world experience. Virtual reality immerses you in a digital experience so your view of a physical space shifts to adapt to a new digital environment. Both these technologies accomplish the goal of simulating a physical experience for students who may not be able to visit a space in real life.

Are these technologies a substitute for the "real thing"? Notwithstanding a few notable exceptions—dissecting a frog via an AR experience may be preferable to physical dissection in your classroom in some instances—AR and VR should not replace a real experience when a real experience is feasible. The value of using this type of technology comes when students are able to experience something they otherwise would not be able to. For example, if your students are learning about ancient Greece and cannot make a trip to the Parthenon, they can access 360-degree panoramas to explore this space. They might access this content on a website like 360cities.net or watch a video tour filmed by a museum docent with a 360-degree camera that has been uploaded to the museum's YouTube channel. Or if your students are learning about the planets in our solar system, they can "hold" a model of Saturn in their hand using Merge Cube's VR technology to spin it around and tap to learn more. This type of interaction with a planet would go above and beyond the experience of reading a paragraph about Saturn in a science textbook.

In my book *Tasks Before Apps* (Burns, 2018), I talk about the power of digital tools, including virtual reality, to spark discussion and push students to question the world around them. Although technology has evolved since the publication of that book, the intention remains the same. Here is an excerpt:

> Our goal on the journey of thoughtful technology integration is to take the best practices of the past to the next level with digital tools. We want to build on the foundation of traditional tasks to empower students as wonderers and answer-seekers. As students inquire about matters both on their own and with our guidance, we can help them come to see tablets, smartphones, and computers as portals to an entire world of innovative problem solving: virtual reality (VR) experiences provoke questions, online search tools bring answers to our fingertips, and videos show how classroom skills are applied in the real world. (p. 43)

Virtual reality might seem flashy and gimmicky on the surface, especially if you have watched viral videos of people with headsets bumping into the wall as they try out a new game in their living room. In an educational setting, educators have the opportunity to integrate VR experiences thoughtfully into instruction to transform how students look at the world. Anchoring these experiences in a clear purpose and setting a learning intention is the best way to get started.

You can apply the strategies for curating resources we explored in Chapter 2 to your decisions on integrating emerging technologies into your instruction. When choosing VR or AR resources to share with students, you might ask yourself, *How might this provide background information to my students? How will this learning experience make the content I teach more memorable? How can we incorporate a discussion to follow up on this experience?*

Virtual Reality Discussion Prompts

Tailor these discussion prompts to the content and learning experience you design for your students.

Observations:

- What do you see?
- What do you hear?
- What time of day is it here?

Wonderings:

- What do you think the weather is like in this place?
- How do you think someone captured this moment?
- What might be missing from this shot?
- What do you think it smells like?
- How would this look different at daytime/nighttime?

Building empathy:

- What might it be like to live in this place?
- How is what you see similar to or different from a place where you have lived?
- Is this a place you would want to visit? Why or why not?
- How far away are we from this place right now?
- How long would it take us to get to this place?

Videoconferencing

Connecting over video is easier than ever, and children and adults of all ages have had more experience with videoconferencing technology as a result of shifts to distance learning in the early 2020s. Videoconferencing connects live video and audio between two or more participants. This type of call often provides a space for participants to share links or text messages using a chat feature. A videoconference differs from a webinar, which typically provides information with a set focus and has multiple attendees viewing at the same time, making the experience feel more passive and impersonal. Videoconferencing lets individuals or groups connect for conversations, interviews, or the sharing of information, such as updates on a project or progress on work toward a common goal. It can help students explore the world and learn from others by "beaming" into another classroom, connecting with a subject-matter expert, or interacting with someone who may be nearby but unable to visit the class to discuss a particular topic. Just as students can use a movie-making tool to create such varied products as a math tutorial or a book trailer, a videoconferencing platform can help you address many different goals.

Videoconferencing is one way to help foster connections outside your classroom or school community. ISTE Student Standard Indicator 1.7.a relates to these Global Connections, stating, "Students use digital tools to connect with learners from a variety of backgrounds and cultures, engaging with them in ways that broaden mutual understanding and learning." When students participate in videoconferences to connect with learners and experts from different corners of the globe, they are exploring with the help of digital tools.

Considerations for Successful Videoconferencing

In Chapter 12, we will talk more about planning for using technology such as videoconferencing to connect with students who may require instruction from outside the classroom during certain points in the school year (e.g., when schools are closed due to inclement weather). Let's look at some basic considerations for successful videoconferencing when exploration is the central goal.

Establishing a purpose. Your primary purpose for hosting a videoconference may fall under the general umbrella of wanting students to have a better understanding of their world. However, you can narrow this goal further to address specific objectives. For example, you may want your elementary school students to "visit" a museum several states away to experience a special exhibit on the Voting Rights Act of 1965. They can participate in a videoconference with a museum docent who uses a mobile device like an iPad to take them around the exhibit to discuss the artifacts on display.

Finding someone to connect with. How do you find a guest expert or a class to connect with for a videoconference? Start off with people you know, including former colleagues, family friends, or organizations your school has partnered with in the past. Expand this circle to reach out to community members or a content-area expert you have located through an online search. For example, you might follow a local food blogger on Instagram who can chat with your class about healthy eating choices during a unit on nutrition. Sending someone a message to ask for 20 minutes of their time may result in a memorable and informative experience for both your students and the subject-matter expert, without the added burden of travel.

Setting students up for success. Ask yourself, *What would make this videoconferencing experience a success?* The answers might vary from one classroom to the next, but in addition to the basic requirement of a strong internet connection, you might view a successful experience as one in which students do the following:

- Develop and ask questions.
- Make a connection to a career.
- Take turns with their classmates.

Setting your guest up for success. Send clear instructions and expectations to your videoconferencing guest. Although they likely have experience using Zoom with their colleagues, interacting virtually with a group of students may be new to them. These instructions might include tips such as double-checking a background space to confirm it is "kid-friendly" or having a pair of headphones nearby to make sure the audio is clear.

Connecting asynchronously. Although we often think of a videoconference as a synchronous or live event, students can also ask and answer questions with a guest speaker in an asynchronous setting. For example, you might have students post questions for a guest speaker over the course of a week by either using a video-recording tool like Flip or adding their questions to a collaborative space like Padlet. Then the guest speaker can

Closed Captioning

Some videoconferencing tools, including Microsoft Teams and Google Meet, have a built-in capacity for live closed captioning. Captioning may be a necessary accommodation for your students or a feature to consider if you are in a learning environment with considerable ambient sound.

record responses to these questions and students can watch the recording at a time that fits their schedule.

Virtual Field Trips and Fostering Curiosity

Providing opportunities for students to explore the world fosters their curiosity. As a classroom teacher in New York City, I loved taking students on field trips, and each year we covered a lot of ground. The list of memorable trips is long, with destinations ranging from the Intrepid Museum and the American Museum of Natural History to the South Street Seaport and the Museum of Modern Art.

Chatbots and Virtual Field Trips

A chatbot can help you gather ideas for virtual field trips. Here are a few prompts to customize:

- My [grade level] students are learning about [topic]. What types of experts can I contact for them to interview?
- I am teaching [grade level] students about [topic]. Our goal is [objective]. What are some unexpected places we can learn about that connect to this topic?
- Make a list of five places students can explore for a virtual field trip that connects to [objective] and [student interest].

One of the most memorable field trips my class of 5th graders took was to the Central Park Zoo the year we started a composting effort in our classroom. As we entered an exhibit hall with plants and animals from the rainforest, one of the students said to me, "It smells just like the composting bin!" She was absolutely right; the humidity and the fresh soil smelled just like the contents of our class compost bin when we lifted the lid. Although we could have virtually visited a farm in California to talk with a farmer or watched a 360 video of an industrial composting process, this in-person field trip was certainly memorable.

Providing students with experiences that allow them to explore their world is essential, but it is not possible to physically take them to every place connected to your curriculum or their interests. The term *virtual field trip* can refer to many things, including a virtual reality experience in which students wear a headset and turn around as they look at a new place from different angles. It could also mean creating a playlist for students with video clips they can watch to learn about a place. The big idea is simple: give students a chance to learn about and explore a place they cannot visit or have not visited in person.

For example, in an elementary classroom, you might open up a panoramic image of a pond on a student tablet or an interactive whiteboard. As you talk to students about the life cycle of a frog, they can see the color of the pond and imagine tadpoles swimming beneath the surface. In a middle school classroom, you might study tessellations with students and send them the link to an interactive walking tour outside the Louvre Museum in Paris. They can move around the Louvre Pyramid and see how tessellations form this massive structure. In a high school classroom, you might have students use a virtual reality headset to walk through parts of the Grand Canyon or Monument Valley. They can see different types of rocks, better understand the scale of these spaces, and make connections to a unit of study on national parks and the Works Progress Administration in a social studies class or to a geology unit in an earth science class.

The purpose for these explorations can be manifold. You may want students to ask questions for further inquiry related to upcoming research projects, or you may want them to write journal entries and reflect on new things they learned and possible connections to lingering or even unanswerable questions. Having students record their thoughts about an experience can help them extend their questions to other parts of their lives and make them more discerning consumers of content.

Asking questions or wondering about something in this way might not come naturally to students. This does not mean they are incapable of asking questions or are not curious; it may just mean they are not used to verbalizing and sharing their wonderings aloud. Students might also hesitate to share if they do not feel comfortable or safe in a particular environment. Creating an open and nonjudgmental space that values questions—even those without an answer—is essential for students of all ages.

The idea of exploration as an essential practice goes hand in hand with the importance of curiosity in the classroom. Modeling this experience for students might include a series of think-aloud questions starting with sentence stems such as these:

- I wonder . . .
- What if . . . ?
- I noticed . . .
- Is it possible to . . . ?
- Could we visit . . . ?
- Who can we talk to about . . . ?
- Where can we go to learn more about . . . ?

Final Thoughts

Exploring the world with students can take many forms and serve a variety of purposes. Whether you want to build content knowledge or help students make connections, the possibilities are truly endless. In the next few chapters, we'll examine how students can collaborate, create, and share their learning experiences. As your students explore the world with the help of digital tools, they can write or record a journal entry, create a video tour, or even design a collage incorporating their favorite things about a particular place. When used with intention, educational technology can open the world to student explorers in any grade level or subject area!

6

Collaborate Across
Digital Spaces

work together, cooperate, combine, team up, partner with, join forces

Collaboration is not unique to a classroom with a cart of Chromebooks or schools where students have access to tablets. Students often participate in collaborative learning experiences without technology, using construction paper and crayons, for example, or building prototypes or models with blocks. Students of all ages work in teams or small groups to accomplish a goal, sitting side by side on the rug or at a table with classmates. Before interactive whiteboards or tablets, students worked together to build on the ideas of their peers, ask and give feedback, and do so much more. Although offline collaboration and learning experiences are important, students must also learn how to **collaborate** in digital spaces.

Students who collaborate are on a mission. They might work on an independent project and need feedback from their classmates. Students might work to solve a math problem from a textbook and solicit the help of a partner, try to unpack an idea from a confusing video and need to ask a clarifying question, or search for a tutorial online. They might need some suggestions or support from students participating in similar learning experiences. Collaboration is more than just working together while sharing the same physical or virtual space. Fostering collaboration in a classroom requires a level of support, trust, and understanding you can cultivate in a tech-rich environment.

Collaboration in a tech-friendly classroom can take many forms. You may have students sitting next to each other in a face-to-face learning environment sharing a screen as they brainstorm ideas and compromise on a decision while working on a podcast together. It could also include times when students log in to an online platform at different parts of the day or from two different locations. Developing structures for tech-friendly collaborations depends on a variety of factors. In this chapter, we'll consider factors such as the ways students currently navigate digital spaces, their primary location for instruction and delivery, and the support they need when navigating online spaces with their classmates.

Why Is This Essential?

In Chapter 5, we examined the social and emotional learning connection to building understanding and empathy through exploration. Revisiting the CASEL framework (CASEL, n.d.) shows clear connections to collaborative learning environments, particularly in terms of relationship skills. If SEL terminology is not incorporated into the mission of your school or district, you may also find your state or national standards incorporate language around collaborative learning and expectations for students.

In addition to these considerations is the need to address the broader issue of the role of collaboration in everyday life. In "The Science Behind the Growing Importance of Collaboration," Emily Stone (2017) details the research and insights of Benjamin F. Jones, the faculty director of the Kellogg Innovation and Entrepreneurship Initiative (KIEI) at Northwestern University. This research examines the future of collaboration and the importance of understanding that, as a result of individuals' knowledge bases becoming more and more specialized, collaboration is increasingly important in every aspect of our lives. Simply put, because individuals know one topic very well, they need to be around other people with specialized knowledge to create a well-rounded plan for solving a problem or addressing a task.

Now, you might be thinking, "My 1st graders [or 6th graders or 11th graders] are not quite experts on a specialized topic—at least not yet." However, you can prepare students for collaborative experiences at an early age, enabling them to strengthen their ability to work toward a common goal with peers at any age. To help you do so, let's take a look at different models for collaboration, the role of peer feedback in your classroom, and how to incorporate productive online discussions into any subject area.

Models for Collaboration

In *Tasks Before Apps* (Burns, 2018), I dedicated a chapter to collaboration and discussed three types of tech-friendly collaboration: *remote, role-based,* and *shared-screen.* In this book, we will look at two more types of collaborative learning experiences—*synchronous* and *asynchronous.* Both can take place within the four walls of a traditional face-to-face classroom, as part of hybrid learning experiences, or during moments when students check in on a project or task at different points in the day. Let's start with the first three: *remote, role-based,* and *shared-screen collaboration.*

Remote, Role-Based, and Shared-Screen Collaboration

In the *remote collaboration* model, students work on individual devices to contribute to a single shared creation. For example, students might create a presentation using Google Slides and log in from their own Chromebooks to add to the slide deck. Students might contribute to the slide deck at the same time or different parts of the day as they add on to the ideas of their classmates. They might chat in real time as they work through a task together, or leave notes and comments.

When engaged in *role-based collaboration,* students work on individual devices to complete assigned tasks for a group project. For example, in a group developing a public service announcement, one student might locate images on a website like Unsplash, another might interview a community member, and a third might create a storyboard. Each student has a specific role, and all three students come together to create the final project.

In *shared-screen collaboration,* students work together in pairs to complete a task using one device. For example, two students might use a single iPad to snap pictures during a community walk, then sit side by side and use a movie-making tool like iMovie or Clips to record their voices and add narration to a slideshow.

It is worth noting that shared-screen collaboration is not only reserved for schools with a limited number of devices. As a classroom teacher with access to iPads for every student, I often asked students to share one device. The benefits were manifold. Student conversations created opportunities for them to compromise, to share, and to defend their opinions and evaluate the positions and arguments of others. Students of all ages can engage in critical thinking skills and participate in these kinds of conversations as they share a screen.

These three models all ask students to work toward a common goal. The tasks and interactions may vary, but all three leverage the power of digital tools to facilitate a collaborative experience for students. The difference between the three lies in the kinds of environments in which they operate. A shared-screen collaboration takes place with students in the same space at the same time; remote and role-based collaboration, by contrast, lend themselves to both *synchronous* and *asynchronous* learning environments.

Synchronous and Asynchronous Collaboration

Synchronous and asynchronous collaboration can take place whether students are sitting side by side or checking in on their work at different times and locations.

In a *synchronous* learning environment, students participate at the same time. When students work together at the same time, they can receive instant feedback (from teachers or classmates) and monitor their progress and the progress of their peers in real time. Synchronous collaboration has numerous benefits for students at all levels. For example, high school or middle school students might contribute to a shared document at the same time as they share a physical workspace, or they might update members of a group at a school on the other side of the district on the progress of a project during a live video call. At the elementary level, students might participate in a whole-class discussion led by their teacher or talk in small groups of their peers to share updates or celebrate accomplishments.

Synchronous collaboration may be limited in distance- and hybrid-learning environments, where students typically make their own schedule or work at their own pace. In these instances, it is important to provide flexibility and understanding for students who may not be able to participate at a scheduled time. This situation requires you to strike a balance between synchronous and asynchronous collaboration.

In an *asynchronous* learning environment, students work through content at different times while adhering to a general schedule or timeline.

For example, a teacher might post a collection of videos or an article for students to read and discuss. There is an expectation students will view the content during a set time frame, but not at an exact time (Burns, 2020a). Students in the class can participate at a time of day or day of the week that works for them depending on the constraints set up for the task by the teacher.

Asynchronous collaboration can happen in blended learning environments where students take ownership of their learning and often work with the support of a small group. This can take place in a station-rotation model, a literature circle or book club, or a student- or teacher-formed study group. When students collaborate asynchronously, they can make their own personal schedule while still meeting the expectations of their group. This option provides an opportunity for students to practice time management and project management skills as they develop a schedule with the input and guidance of a teacher, coach, or counselor.

In Chapter 12 ("Plan for Tech-Rich Learning Experiences"), we'll examine these models of collaboration from an educator perspective and explore what collaborative experiences can look like for educators who work in teams to plan instruction and interventions for students.

> **Spaces for Collaboration**
> Educator and EdTech expert Rachelle Dené Poth (2023) describes the value of creating spaces for students to collaborate: "At the beginning of each school year, educators can start with icebreakers and use class activities to get to know their students better and help students to learn about and connect with one another" (para. 3). She describes how teachers can incorporate a mix of digital tools with hands-on activities. You can hear more from Rachelle in my (2023c) *Easy EdTech Podcast*, where she shares activities that can help students reflect on the way they interact in digital spaces. To listen, scan the QR code.
>
>
>
> *Easy EdTech Podcast*: 219

Peer Feedback

When working in digital spaces, students can give and receive feedback on their work while sitting side by side in a shared-screen environment, looking over their partner's shoulder to offer support. Students can also give and receive feedback when they log in to the same space as a classmate synchronously or asynchronously. A pair of 9th grade students from schools in two different time zones can participate in a video chat as they review each other's feedback on their science research, or a 3rd grader can open up their interactive journal and listen to the audio comments left by a classmate while they were working in a reading group with their teacher.

Student feedback is an important component of collaboration in digital spaces. (In Chapter 8, we will look at assessment and feedback from a teacher's perspective of checking for understanding with digital tools.) Students should be able to give, receive, and act on feedback in online environments as well as in face-to-face conversations with their teachers and peers. Let's take a closer look at what feedback can look like in a digital space as students give feedback to classmates, and when they review and then act on the feedback they have received from peers.

Giving Feedback

Online Feedback Tips to Share with Students

- Reread your comment before submitting to make sure your tone is clear (or use an audio recording instead).

- Include an action item or a question to help your classmate think about a next step.

- Put yourself in your classmate's shoes and decide if this comment is helpful and productive.

- Include an emoji along with your comment, such as a thumbs-up or a smiley face to show your support.

Students can give feedback to one another during a wide range of activities. By establishing norms and reviewing examples of useful feedback, you can help set them up for success. You might introduce a system you revisit throughout the year, such as a *glow and grow* (*glow* is feedback on a strength, while *grow* is feedback on an area in need of improvement). A student might reference indicators on a rubric to give feedback for each of these two categories. Alternatively, you might ask students to use sentence starters such as "One thing I noticed . . ." or "One thing I wondered . . ."

Peer feedback can happen throughout the school day and is not just for digital spaces. However, you can build on feedback structures students are already comfortable using and transfer these offline experiences to online spaces. There are a few best practices for peer feedback specific to online spaces. For example, if students will leave comments on a piece of student work as peer feedback, it is important to distinguish this action from how students might typically think about leaving comments on social media. Although we might appreciate the difference between leaving a comment on an Instagram photo of someone's vacation and leaving a comment to provide valuable, actionable feedback, students might conflate these two types of comments and need support in identifying the difference. To reinforce this idea, you might share with students examples of comments that fall into the categories *nice* versus *helpful*. When students give feedback on the work of their classmates, it should be specific and provide clear value.

Encourage students to get specific. A comment left by one student on another student's work should be clear and concise. Encourage students to highlight a line of text they are referring to or place a digital sticky note on a particular item or element of their classmate's work. Students can also leave comments that reference a particular part of a project. For example, students giving feedback on a video project might mention the time stamp they are referring to, such as "At minute 2:25 you include a great picture of the setting of your book. You might want to include more photos earlier in the video to make sure the viewer understands where the book takes place." To illustrate this concept, you might share examples with students of comments that are specific and comments that aren't specific enough to take action.

Explain how to share a recommendation. One of the benefits of working in digital spaces is the interactivity it provides. A recommendation can go beyond the quick comment we might jot down with a pencil on a paper sticky note. Instead, students can leave recommendations with links to additional resources. A student might share a link to a helpful website or video with their classmate, or a recommendation of an online resource related to the project. Just as you might model how students can be specific with their feedback, you can model how to share a recommended resource before sending students off to provide feedback to their peers. For example, you can show your class how you might suggest a resource to a student working on a public service announcement about endangered species. You might model leaving a comment such as this: "I like how you talked about your animal's habitat. Here is a resource I used to learn more about my animal's habitat that might help you, too: www .worldwildlife.org."

Comment Buddies

In a digital space, making sure everyone has received feedback from their classmates is challenging without a clear structure in place. Establish "comment buddies" by creating groups of three or four students who will comment on one another's work. This ensures everyone knows whom to give feedback to. Once they have left comments on the work of their buddies, students can explore the work of the rest of their classmates.

Receiving and Acting on Feedback

The process of receiving feedback in digital spaces may in some ways feel similar to the process of receiving nondigital feedback. Instead of sorting through sticky notes of feedback scattered throughout a notebook or skimming the notes left by a classmate in the margins of their paper, however, students will receive feedback in a digital space that requires a special set of navigational skills. Here are a few key differences in the ways students can receive and act on digital feedback.

Prioritizing action items. If students open up a document with a large number of comments from a classmate, you might encourage them to review all the feedback at once before taking action. After they review the feedback, students can construct a plan of action to help them prioritize their next steps. For example, a 6th grader might open a document she created with questions she has drafted for an interview with a city councilperson. She might see multiple comments left by classmates with suggestions on how to tweak the questions or with more questions to add to her list.

In general, when students have a lot of comments to sort through, encourage them to do the following:

1. First, read all comments and dismiss any that are not helpful or very useful.
2. Next, decide which comments are high-priority and which are low-priority.
3. Then, if necessary, reach out to the commenter with any clarifying questions.
4. Finally, make a list of things to address or take action on.

Responding to clarify or offer thanks. In the same way we want to make sure a sticky note with a comment does not fall off a sheet of paper, we do not want to lose track of digital feedback spread across a document. Navigating a document with many comments requires practice, and you can explain how to handle a set of comments by modeling your thought processes and actions. Pull up a document with comments so students can watch your thought process as you navigate this space. Demonstrate how you think about a comment you received and whether you want to take the advice given to you or perhaps ask for clarification. Model any other navigational steps particular to the tool you are using with your class, such as how to resolve or dismiss comments that are no longer necessary or relevant.

Students can acknowledge the feedback they received from a classmate with a "thank you" on a comment thread. They might also accept feedback by sharing a way they took action based on the comment a student left. This acknowledgment provides an opportunity for students in the role of commenter to see how their feedback helped someone else and how the time they allocated for providing feedback was useful and well received. For example, a 2nd grade student might open his Seesaw account to look at comments on a video he created in which he labeled parts of a flower. He might see a comment left by a classmate asking him a question about the flower, which he can reply to on the comment thread. These exchanges may happen organically between students without any explicit instruction, especially for older students who may have experience navigating social spaces and online discussion threads. Because every student's exposure to these types of online interactions is different, you will want to allocate time to model these skills for students and provide time for them to practice leaving comments on their classmates' work.

The Value-Add of Audio and Video Feedback

Have you ever received a text message where you weren't sure of the sender's emotions, even if the sender was a family member or friend? When reading such a text, you might have had trouble figuring out the sender's tone, wondering whether they were frustrated, upset, or joking—even if the most likely answer was that they were walking into the supermarket, rushing between meetings, or trying the voice-to-text feature on their phone for the first time. Even with the people closest to us, text-only messages can be difficult to decipher. Now imagine a similar scenario for a student who has read a comment on their work from a classmate or teacher and is not quite sure of the tone. If they were not very confident when they submitted their work in the first place or are in the middle of a tough day, that student may misinterpret a text-only comment as harsh or unsupportive, even if that was the opposite of the commenter's intended tone. In such cases, an audio or video comment would have been more effective.

Audio and video responses address several goals related to student feedback. First, audio and video feedback helps communicate tone. Students can hear and see their classmate's or teacher's energy and encouragement in the response. These elements may be lost in a text-only message. This type of feedback can help students feel heard and supported. It provides a way to communicate a suggestion, a piece of advice, or an action item alongside the enthusiasm of the person giving feedback.

Audio and video feedback also offers a level of ease and efficiency for both teachers and students. Whether it is a teacher giving feedback to a student or a student giving feedback to a classmate, giving

Tools for Audio and Video Feedback

- Flip: an app that allows video responses in a collaborative space

- Mote: a Google Docs and Slides add-on enabling voice comments

- Padlet: a digital tool with options for adding voice notes to a shared space

- Seesaw: a classroom app allowing comments on posts to be given in text and audio format

an audio or video response is often a quicker way of communicating. In the case of teachers, providing feedback to students more quickly means you can reallocate the time you save to other tasks, such as designing supports and interventions based on formative assessment data you might collect in the process of observing student peer feedback loops.

Productive Online Discussions

Creating opportunities for productive online discussions requires strategy and planning. Some students may be familiar with communicating in digital spaces, like using a gaming tool with a chat feature. Other students may be new to the idea of chatting and communicating in online spaces. Your goals for tech-friendly discussions may be manifold, including building classroom community and establishing channels for collaboration both inside and outside the classroom. At the heart of a productive online discussion is an opportunity for students to connect, apply what they have learned, and work together with a common goal in mind.

Types of Tech-Friendly Discussions

A tech-friendly discussion leverages the unique features of digital spaces and builds on the foundation of traditional, face-to-face communication. It is not a substitute for this type of interaction; instead, it can add value to the experiences students may already have corresponding and connecting with their classmates. To truly be prepared to survive and excel in our changing world, students must know how to communicate and collaborate in online discussions.

There are different types of tech-friendly discussions that promote collaboration and use the features of a variety of tools. However, they are not necessarily independent of one another and may share certain features and implementation models.

Synchronous discussions take place at a set time and may include video and audio conversations as well as chat spaces. Tools for such discussions include Zoom, Google Meet, and Microsoft Teams.

Asynchronous discussions take place over a set period of time, and are not live. Students can jump in and out and build on comments left by other students. Tools for this type of discussion include Blackboard, PowerSchool Schoology Learning, and Flip.

Text-based discussions use text communication primarily or entirely, including long responses consisting of several sentences or paragraphs, or short responses consisting of phrases or a single sentence. Video-conferencing tools such as Google Meet and Zoom have chat spaces where text-based discussions can take place in addition to a video call.

Video-based discussions can feature students appearing on video for a live conversation or have students submit videos with their responses for classmates to view on their own time. Tools for live videoconferencing include Microsoft Teams and FaceTime; video posting tools include Flip and Seesaw.

Audio-based discussions feature students on a live call without video capability or students submitting prerecorded audio with responses for their classmates to listen to on their own time. Tools for live conferencing using audio include Zoom and Google Meet; students can use tools like Soundtrap and Padlet to post audio responses.

Throughout their interactions with peers in online spaces, students are often working toward a common goal. This could include providing feedback, asking for support, or completing a task together. ISTE Student Standard Indicator 1.7.c, Project Teams, addresses this aspect of online collaboration; it states, "Students contribute constructively to project teams, assuming various roles and responsibilities to work effectively toward a common goal."

Establishing a Purpose

Although the purpose of a discussion forum might be obvious to you, students may not see the value of using an online space for discussion without clearly communicated goals. Establishing a purpose before introducing a new discussion space or inviting students to join the conversation in a video call is essential. The idea of setting a purpose for a discussion is not unique to tech-friendly learning experiences; this happens when elementary students gather on the rug and when middle and high school students break into small groups to talk about a question posed to the class. In a digital space, you will want to build on the traditional best practices associated with classroom discussion and share the goals for a discussion with students. You might establish the purpose of a live videoconference with a visual on your screen to remind students of the goals for the session, or you might include the goals in your directions for a self-paced activity students will participate in without your in-person or side-by-side support.

For example, in a 1st grade classroom, you might say, "Today in our video call, our goal is to hear what our classmates loved most, or didn't like so much, about the read-aloud book. This discussion can help us figure out who we can go to when we are looking for book recommendations and help us think more about the characters in the book." In a 10th grade classroom, you might post instructions for students in a discussion forum to remind them that the purpose is to share ideas for future inquiry projects and help their classmates dig deeper into a topic they would like to learn more about.

Setting Norms and Expectations

In any classroom space, setting norms and expectations is crucial for student success. As a 5th grade classroom teacher, I had many silly routines with my students, including ones we used for discussion. One favorite, which was borrowed from a fantastic 4th grade teacher in my school, asked students to tap their heads to signal when they agreed with the speaker. It was a way for them to employ active-listening skills and let their classmates know where they stood on an issue.

You can create a list of expectations together with your students so everyone is on the same page and has thought about the *why* of an expectation before being asked to adopt it. Here are a few examples:

- In a discussion forum, we choose emojis carefully and use just one or two for any comment we leave.
- On a video call, we raise our hand when we want to unmute ourselves and jump into the discussion, or share an idea by typing it into the chat area.
- In a breakout video session or small group, we can take turns sharing ideas and place helpful links in a chat space.
- When sharing in a discussion space, we add starter words or hashtags like #Question, #Idea, #Resource, or #Ask to help our contributions to the conversation stand out and stay organized.

Collaboration with Chatbots

Merriam-Webster (n.d.) defines *collaborate* as "to work jointly with others or together especially in an intellectual endeavor." With an AI mindset, we can expand our conception of "others" to include the support one can receive from generative AI. In Chapters 3 and 4, we examined how artificial intelligence tools can help educators generate instructional content and the importance of helping students understand how to evaluate content in digital spaces with AI in mind. Educators may already view chatbots like ChatGPT or Gemini as collaborators in developing instructional materials for their students. As they look toward the future, students, too, will increasingly need to view this technology as a collaborator in their work.

In a working paper from the Harvard Business School examining the impact of AI in the workforce, the authors "suggest that the capabilities of AI create a 'jagged technological frontier' where some tasks are easily done by AI, while others, though seemingly similar in difficulty level, are outside the current capability of AI" (Dell'Acqua et al., 2023, p. 2). The implications of these findings are clear for the education arena. For certain tasks where students crave guidance and feedback throughout the creative process, generative AI can offer support. Although this technology is not perfect or currently accessible to all students, it is certainly an area worth watching in the context of collaboration.

Chatbots as Co-Learners and Helpers

When used by students in an educational setting, chatbots can act as co-learners and helpers. Tutoring in offline and online spaces is far from new. Students have worked with tutors to foster a co-learning experience as they review material, practice skills, and explore new content. Now chatbot technology has entered the conversation around individualized student support. Tools like Khanmigo from Khan Academy are designed specifically for school use to act as teaching assistants and virtual tutors inside and outside the classroom. This type of AI-powered tool can prompt students to think step-by-step when solving a problem and guide them toward the answer.

Although chatbots like ChatGPT are not COPPA-compliant, students might still use these tools at home to support their learning. They might also use student-friendly tools with generative AI components, such as Canva or Adobe Express. Students can use generative AI to jump-start ideas and inspiration as part of the design process, instead of as a substitute for their creative process—a topic we'll look at in the next chapter. For example, 1st graders might discuss and decide on a prompt to submit to an image generation tool to help them create a design that complements a more traditional writing experience. Their teacher might add the students' prompt to a tool like Adobe Firefly and share the final product with students. Or a group of high school students might use a chatbot tool to generate a list of ideas for a research project and choose one on the list to investigate further.

As this space evolves, you may find yourself taking on the role of a co-learner with students while exploring the impact of chatbots as helpers. Although it doesn't specifically mention co-learning about artificial intelligence, ISTE Educator Standard 2.4, Collaborator, specifically Indicator 2.4.b, Learn Alongside Students, encourages educators to "Collaborate and co-learn with students to discover and use new digital resources, and diagnose and troubleshoot technology issues." This might include exploring the role of chatbots as co-learners and helpers.

Final Thoughts

Collaboration plays a crucial role in student interactions throughout the school day. Students can work together toward a common goal in small moments and leverage the features of digital tools to provide timely, actionable feedback to their classmates. Starting the school year with clear structures that support collaborative learning, or introducing new procedures midyear, requires the same investment needed for adopting any new routine. This commitment to collaborative learning will help strengthen your classroom community as students work together and support their peers throughout the school year.

7

Create Multimodal Artifacts of Learning

---

make, generate, yield, produce, catalyze, result in

Students create in both big and small ways throughout the school year. From a high schooler crafting a caption to accompany a social media post to an elementary school student selecting the perfect color for an illustration, creation takes many forms. Students' creations are not limited to social media posts or drawings, of course. These creations can span a wide range of products similar to the ones they consume as readers, listeners, and viewers. In this chapter, we will examine how to support students as creators in digital spaces in the age of AI. We will look at how to develop the supporting resources necessary for everyday artifacts of student learning as well as for larger independent and collaborative projects.

In all classroom settings, students need time and space to create products to capture and share their learning. Students can synthesize information, apply what they have learned in a relevant context, and share this learning with an audience. In later chapters, we will dive into strategies for assessing student work, sharing student work, and establishing an audience for their learning. In this chapter, we will look at *what* students can **create** within digital spaces and *how* to set them up for success as creators. We'll look at the impact of AI on student creativity as well as the use of AI tools to support educators as they develop instructional resources, like checklists and exemplars, for their students.

Why Is This Essential?

Often when we think of creativity in the classroom, our first thought is of art projects involving paintbrushes or construction paper. But creativity is an important part of almost everything we do and extends well beyond the art classroom. "Getting creative" is an essential part of any type of problem-solving activity and a key component of how we apply what we have learned. In tech-friendly environments, student creators can use digital tools to capture ideas, organize information, and create an artifact of their learning. The ability to create in a digital space is an essential skill in every subject area.

Students working within digital spaces need experience using a variety of media—voice, text, images, and more—to create an artifact of their learning. Digital media might include a presentation tool that enables students to design slides to share their learning as well as a word-processing platform where a student's creation might include more text than other media. However, there are many different ways for students to create a digital product. We can take students beyond a traditional presentation or publishing method for their work and incorporate a variety of digital features. In a tech-friendly classroom, this effort can take many forms. For example, students could create quick 15-second videos to chronicle the steps they used to solve an algebra problem or to share the facts they have learned about an animal inspired by videos on TikTok or Instagram Reels. Or students might create audio recordings in which they interview a classmate or a subject-matter expert inspired by kid-friendly podcasts such as *Wow in the World* or *Brains On!*

Sir Ken Robinson (2006) shared in his iconic TED Talk how "creativity now is as important in education as literacy, and we should treat it with the same status." Creativity in digital spaces asks students to employ higher-order thinking skills such as analyzing, synthesizing, and evaluating information as they create something new. Although student research on a topic such as polar bears might not include a trip to the Arctic Circle or conclude with a completely new discovery, the learning artifact students create—a slideshow of facts, a podcast interviewing an ecologist—did not exist before they compiled this information to create a new piece of work. Students may not pursue future careers as graphic designers or podcast producers, but the skills they gather as they create are transferable to many environments outside the classroom.

ISTE Student Standard 1.6 is all about helping students communicate their learning creatively. Indicator 1.6.b, Original and Remixed Works, states, "Students create original works or responsibly repurpose or remix digital resources into new creations." In this chapter, we explore how students can create artifacts of learning using digital tools in a variety of ways. As we consider the implications of easily accessible generative AI tools, conversations on creativity in the classroom may increase attention to the "remixed works" aspect of this indicator.

Creativity in the Age of AI

Will computers, robots, and artificial intelligence replace humans? You've probably heard some version of this question during the last few decades, and the rapid adoption of AI-powered technology has placed this concern front and center in education. Although there are several schools of thought on this topic, I am interested to see the continued influence of AI in this space, both in classrooms and more widely. The following are a few broad considerations you can apply to creativity in the classroom.

Broad Considerations for Creativity and AI

In the *Journal of Creative Behavior*, creativity researchers (Vinchon et al., 2023) describe the intersection of artificial intelligence and creativity this way: "AI has proven to be an effective aid during parts of the creative process. However, humans do not appear to be at risk of being effectively eliminated from the process as they assume higher-level decision-making roles (e.g., which questions to ask, how to refine questions, which part of the text to keep, which image to change, etc., which production is finally chosen)" (para. 16). The authors use the term *Co-cre-AI-tion* to describe a possible future they describe as a "real collaborative effort involving more or less equally the human and the generative AI, with recognition of the contributions of each party" (para. 18).

One of the common arguments in favor of the power of AI is its ability to automate and accelerate everyday tasks. In an article for the World Economic Forum, digitalization and sustainability expert Jan Bieser (2023) describes how "freeing up time is arguably one of AI's greatest contributions to human creativity" (para. 13) as long as it doesn't become a distraction. With this time for creativity, a person who opens up a generative AI tool still needs to have a basic understanding of what types of tasks it can complete.

In an article for the *Harvard Business Review* titled "How Generative AI Can Augment Human Creativity," Eapen and colleagues (2023) share ways generative AI can positively affect the creative process for professionals in various industries. They describe how generative AI can make associations between concepts we might not see as connected to promote divergent thinking and challenge expertise bias by generating unexpected ideas when an expert might not be able to move past their traditional way of thinking. In addition to helping generate ideas, the authors also emphasized how generative AI can promote feedback—an important part of the creative process—and help refine ideas so they address specific constraints. Industries where creative professionals move through a design thinking process are tackling the different ways generative AI will shape their work.

Classroom Considerations for AI's Impact on Creativity

With these broad considerations in mind, what is the role of AI in a 2nd, 6th, or 11th grade classroom? Today's students will likely interact with AI in some fashion in the workforce, and they will increasingly have opportunities as student creators to choose if and when to use generative AI tools in their work. The following are three areas where you can introduce students to AI alongside their role as creator in the classroom. Please keep in mind, some tools using generative AI technologies may be available for students to use independently, whereas others might be best for teachers to model for students.

Generate and evaluate ideas. Demonstrate to students how you can use a prompt to make a list of ideas, such as "Topics a 7th grade student might research about polar bears." Share the list of ideas a chatbot generates with students and model for students how you evaluate the responses. You might share your thoughts or pose the following questions for students to discuss with partners:

- Are these strong, high-quality responses? How do you know?
- What is missing from this list? Is there something I should have included in my prompt?
- Did one of these make you think of a different idea? How did you get from *A* to *B*?

Write and refine prompts. Work together with students to create prompts that will help them generate content. These could include a query for a list of ideas for questions for an interview they are conducting with an expert, a description for an image that complements a creative writing project, or a list of pros and cons related to a concept. You might model the process of writing a prompt, reflecting on the output, and refining the prompt so you get the desired result.

Highlight the process over the final product. For students who are curious as to whether generative AI chatbots like ChatGPT can "do their homework," you may want to introduce classroom routines that place greater emphasis on celebrating the creative process than rewarding the final product. For example, you might already carve out time for peer feedback, but to highlight the creative process you can also allocate time for students to share a "win" from a peer feedback session with the rest of their classmates. You might also decide to have students document their creative process by recording reflection videos, snapping pictures, or journaling to capture their process. These types of products could become part of a celebration for a final piece of student work.

There are many ways to check for understanding, and the next chapter will unpack strategies for formative assessment. ISTE Educator Standard Indicator 2.7.a, Offer Alternative Assessments, demonstrates the importance of providing options for students (including those we explore throughout this chapter), stating, "Provide alternative ways for students to demonstrate competency and reflect on their learning using technology."

Types of Tech-Enhanced Student Creations

The use of digital tools in a classroom setting provides many options for students to create a product of their learning in audio, text, visual, or

multimedia format. Starting with an end product in mind is an important component of students' creative process, and teachers can share
expectations, exemplars, and supporting resources at the beginning of a
creative endeavor. Establishing an audience for student creations is an
important consideration at the start of any creation process, big or small.
Your students might create something that is published for the world to
see at the end of a multiweek exploration of a new topic, or they might
make something at the end of a single lesson to share out with their
classmates for a smaller celebration. In Chapter 10, we will look more at
connecting student work to an audience.

One of the benefits of introducing digital tools to students is the
ability to incorporate multimodal learning experiences into the creative
process. *Multimodal learning* engages students in multiple ways, through
reading, writing, recording, building, drawing, and more. When presenting students with creative opportunities, you can give them options on
how to share their learning. Many digital tools provide more than one
choice for students to create a learning artifact. Let's unpack the different kinds of tech-enhanced creations you may want to introduce to
students.

Audio Creations

An audio creation can take numerous forms. These types of student
products tend to lean heavily on the use of student voice through narration, conversation, and explanation. An audio recording might include a
simple voice caption on a piece of work a student uploads to a common
space (such as when students post a picture to Seesaw and record their
voices to explain it). It could also include a multiweek project in which
students interview three experts on a single topic and create a podcast
to share the interviews, bracketed by an introduction and a conclusion.
As with more traditional student projects, the scope and expectations of
an audio creation can vary.

The goal of an audio recording is to get students to talk about their
own ideas and share what they have learned while providing a clear value-
add or benefit that would not be possible without the use of this technology. For example, you might have students who are conversationally
proficient in the primary language of instruction but who struggle to compose written sentences. This barrier might prevent them from sharing
what they have learned and erode their confidence and enthusiasm for

the content. With an audio recording, students can capture and share what they have learned and build confidence to interact in other spaces. If students are already consumers of audio-based media such as podcasts, they can see a clear connection to a product relevant to their own lives. If your students have not been exposed to this medium, you may want to introduce them to student-friendly podcasts on a high-interest topic.

Before beginning to create an audio-based product, students should have had experience as consumers of this medium. Set a vision for students' own audio products and share examples. If students will create podcasts, you might ask them to listen to clips of podcast episodes as a way to provide context. Reviewing examples together can lead to more productive discussions about what their project will look and sound like.

When students create audio products, they might work with a script or a set of notes to remember key points. A script or clear outline is an important part of an audio-based project and may be something you include in a peer- or teacher-feedback routine. As students get ready to record their own audio-based project, share helpful tips such as finding a quiet place to record, referring to a script or an outline, practicing before hitting the record button, and using headphones or a microphone.

If students do not write a script, they may decide to generate a written transcript of their recording to share in tandem with the digital component of their project. Students will want to make sure their work is accessible to an audience of all their peers, including students, families, and community members. Providing a transcript of an audio project (or adding captions to a video project) can help address this issue. We will talk more about sharing student work in Chapter 9.

Student-Created Podcasts

A podcast gives students a space to talk about their learning. They can create a product that mirrors a popular medium, in the form of a solo voice recording, an interview, or a discussion with another classmate. If students are not familiar with podcasts, it is important to introduce them to this type of media and share a handful of different examples. Students can turn their writing into a podcast by recording themselves reading it aloud, or they can use this medium in place of something more traditional.

A student podcast can accomplish a variety of goals in your classroom. You might want to increase the options for students to share what they have learned about a topic or give them the option to create a product connected to a type of media they already consume. Students can create a podcast lasting just a few minutes or as part of a series; there are many options for customizing this experience for students. Popular tools for student podcasters include Soundtrap and GarageBand.

If you are curious about podcasting in the classroom, go to https://info.iste .org/iste-jumpstart-guides to find the ISTE Jump Start Guide *Podcasting for Students* by Michele Haiken (2020). Michele and I also spoke about the power of introducing creative classroom projects in my (2023d) *Easy EdTech Podcast* (to listen, scan the QR code).

Easy EdTech Podcast: 221

Here are some examples of tools students can use for audio creations:

- Soundtrap for Education
- GarageBand
- Zoom (audio-only recording)
- Adobe Podcast

Text Creations

A text-based product created in an online space provides opportunities for students to use digital tools throughout the writing process and share their written work with the world more easily. The many benefits of working in a digital space go beyond the simple act of word processing and include access to resources and tools that help students review their writing (e.g., Grammarly), connect with a classmate for feedback (e.g., Google Docs), and share early iterations of their work with their teacher (e.g., an LMS such as Canvas, PowerSchool Schoology Learning, or LMS365 in Microsoft Teams).

In addition to tools used to facilitate feedback loops and support the general workflow of students working in a digital space, specific features such as voice-to-text can help students record their thinking and build confidence as writers. Text-based creations using technology go beyond the traditional research paper or writing assignment. Instead of typing up and printing out a product to share with a teacher, students can use various online tools to create a learning artifact that mirrors the type of online content they currently consume. The options are numerous and include content like blog posts, news articles, and interviews as well as microblogging products such as the short (or lengthy) captions found on social media posts.

When guiding students in creating a text-based product, it is important to distinguish between tools geared toward the process of writing—allowing users to easily generate ideas, create a draft, and solicit feedback—and tools more focused on publishing a final product. For example, your students might start off working in a space such as Google Docs or Microsoft Word, where it is easier for them to highlight, leave a comment, or move text around on their screen. Making these changes in a tool designed primarily to share a final product such as Microsoft Sway or the web page–building option in Adobe Express may be more difficult. To illustrate this concept further, think of a writer's workshop where students might first write in a notebook to gather ideas, add sticky notes to a draft page, and cross out sentences they want to eliminate.

Then they shift to "publishing-quality" paper when they are ready to pull everything together into a final, shareable piece of work.

Here are some examples of tools students can use for text-based products:

- Adobe Express
- Microsoft Sway
- Google Sites

Visual Creations

The category of visual creations includes infographics, comic books, sketchnotes (notes with visual elements such as drawings and symbols), illustrations, and more. This type of creation will likely include text, but the visual component is the primary feature. Let's dive into two of these visual products—infographics and comic books—to spotlight ways in which students can use these creations to capture and share their learning.

Infographics

An infographic is a popular medium featured in both print and digital formats. It can help students represent their thinking with visuals including a combination of icons, images, and text set in a thematic color palette. As a visual representation of information, an infographic lends itself well to many types of student learning experiences. It pushes students to think about the organization of their information within a graphic, how to communicate information to an audience, and how data points are an important part of telling a story about a topic. Students can use infographics to represent information they have been given (e.g., a list of data points from the U.S. Geological Survey), data they have found through their own research, and results they have gathered through surveys. Infographics require students to go beyond the surface level of information and organize facts and data into a visual format. This type of student product requires critical thinking and can incorporate collaborative opportunities such as peer feedback. You might ask students to use a template you have created and shared with them, search for a template to modify, or start from scratch.

Comic strips

Comic strips are visual representations that emphasize sequencing of events, making them a great choice for both explanatory and narrative writing. In addition to a topical focus, like retelling a moment from history or breaking down the steps of a science experiment, you can make sure students address English language arts concepts, such as including introductions or conclusions or using precise language to describe a concept. Students can work within a set format for their comic strip or use a template with spots for them to add pictures, captions, and action words within each cell. A student creation like a comic strip requires students to think about visual representation over a series of events or steps, and they can benefit from reviewing examples and discussing the goals of their creation.

In Chapter 1, we looked at ways for students to organize information as they navigate digital spaces. Other options in this category of visual creations are learning artifacts like mind maps, sketchnotes, and graphic organizers, all of which ask students to organize information in a visual format.

Here are some examples of tools students can use for visual creations:

- Canva for Education
- Adobe Express
- PicCollage
- Keynote
- Genially

Multimedia Creations

With clear connections to the audio, visual, and text-based creations described earlier in this chapter, multimedia creations refer to student work products that include a combination of media. A multimedia creation has overlapping benefits, like the student work products discussed in the previous sections. These multimodal artifacts of learning encourage students to combine a variety of media and make the most of all the available features of digital tools. Examples include a slideshow incorporating a combination of pictures, icons, music, and voice, and an ebook with interactive experiences for readers, such as buttons to press to hear a student's voice alongside paragraphs of text or student-selected images related to the topic.

Multimedia projects lend themselves well to environments where students have the option to choose how to present their learning. They give educators a lot of flexibility in supporting the needs of individuals or small groups of students who have access to the same digital tools. For example, you might have an assignment in which all students are asked to create an ebook to chronicle the obstacles they faced completing a science experiment. Half of the students might choose to share their stories with videos embedded in the pages of their ebook, while the others choose to write two paragraphs and add a picture to go along with their writing. Your expectations remain the same, but the output from students may vary.

Access to multimedia tools may leave students feeling both happy to have various options and overwhelmed by the prospect of facing a "blank canvas" for the creations. You may want to share a structure for students to use as a foundation to build on, like a template for their project. Alternatively, you might share more examples than you typically would when introducing a new project to demonstrate to students the variety of creations they may make. For example, imagine a group of 3rd graders asked to create videos to introduce themselves to their classmates. With a video-creation tool, the students could go in many directions to share their favorite things and talk about their interests. You can give students some structure to help them stay focused while still providing options for them to share. You might start by suggesting they include (1) a title slide, (2) a statement about how to pronounce their name, and (3) a goal they have for the school year. Even though you might give students a suggested structure, at the same time, you can give them flexibility to choose images or icons for their visuals, add captions or record their voice, and choose background colors and music to accompany their "all about me" video.

Here are some examples of tools students can use for multimedia products:

- iMovie
- Flip
- Clips
- Book Creator
- Adobe Express

Open-Ended Creation Tools

Open-ended is the term I use to describe an EdTech tool that gives students a blank canvas on which to create. For example, Adobe Express is a tool students could use for creating math tutorials, public service announcements, or infographics with facts about a favorite animal. Bottom line:

there is more than one way to use an open-ended creation tool, and these tools provide students and teachers with many options for creative products. As someone who provides professional development support to educators ranging from kindergarten teachers to high school instructors, I love having tools in my EdTech tool belt that are flexible for a variety of learning environments—and this is where open-ended creation tools come into play.

In *Tasks Before Apps* (Burns, 2018), I shared some guiding questions to help educators determine whether a particular tool is the best fit for a student creator. I have added a few more considerations, resulting in the following list:

- Will students need to record video or take pictures to complete the activity?
- Is the tool web-based, or will students need to download an app or extension?
- Does the tool let students layer features on top of one another (e.g., text on top of images)?
- Can the tool help students create a final product they can easily share with an audience?
- Does the tool supply access to a library of images, or will students need to provide their own?
- Can we use this tool for another project this year, or is this project-specific?
- Is there a colleague who has experience using this tool to whom I can reach out for support?

Creating with (and Without) Digital Tools

Although this book is focused on education technology and working with students in digital spaces, you should not eliminate analog or offline creations from the options you provide for students' next project. There are numerous ways students can combine online and offline experiences. For example, students might use an iPad to snap pictures as they build a compost bin in a community garden, chronicling the process from start to finish and showing how the project connects to their math goals (measurement) and science goals (the food chain). Similarly, you might give students options for creating a scale model of Chichén Itzá, leading some to use Tinkercad to build a 3D model and others to use papier mâché. Digital products do not have to be separate from hands-on experiences and can often add a layer to traditional student creations by capturing the process and celebrating student accomplishments.

Addressing Differing Needs by Differentiating Process and Product

As mentioned earlier, the use of technology with student creators offers considerable added value and plenty of opportunities for student choice. Digital tools can also help you meet your goals for differentiation by addressing the needs of students throughout the creative process.

In *How to Differentiate Instruction in Academically Diverse Classrooms,* Carol Ann Tomlinson (2017) states, "In a differentiated classroom, the teacher assumes that different learners have differing needs and proactively plans lessons that provide a variety of ways to 'get at' and express learning" (p. 5). Tomlinson goes on to describe the importance of three core areas: "(1) **content**—input, what students learn; (2) **process**—how students go about making sense of ideas and information; and (3) **product**—output, or how students demonstrate what they have learned" (p. 7). Previously in this book, we looked at curation as a means of differentiating *content* for students. As students create artifacts of their learning, the *process* of interacting with content and the *products* they create as evidence of learning can further this differentiation.

Value-Add

There are many ways teachers can use technology to unlock the potential of students who may have difficulty showing what they know in traditional ways. When reviewing the features of an open-ended creation tool, identify the value-add, or the possible benefits, in terms of both process and product. For example, in terms of *process,* students who are conversationally proficient in English and working on building their writing skills can benefit from voice-to-text technology; the availability of an audio option might help students share their learning better when they record their voices; and the ease of a voice-to-text search option can help students use vocabulary words to find "just right" images for their project. As you decide on a specific *product* you have in mind for student creations, you might focus on the value-add of different tech-friendly experiences and how the benefits of different features—perhaps a video option in addition to a text option—will set students up for success.

Creating Digital Books

When working with teachers and students, I love introducing and using open-ended creation tools. I had the chance to visit Kōkua Academy on the Big Island of Hawaii and work with elementary students as they were about to kick off a thematic unit on sea creatures. To help students flex their curiosity muscles, we created "I Wonder…" books in which students could capture their questions. For this activity, we used Book Creator, and I encouraged students to use different features of their choice (e.g., pen tool to draw, voice recording to capture audio) as they gathered questions for a future research project. You can read a recap of the activity and find pictures and examples in a post I wrote (2022c) for Book Creator's blog (scan the QR code).

"I Wonder…" Books

Student Choice

In *Learning to Choose, Choosing to Learn,* Mike Anderson (2016) states, "One of the main purposes of choice is to provide a few options for students and have them *self-differentiate*" (p. 6). Anderson emphasizes the importance of student choice and how it can "also combat student apathy, helping students connect with their strengths and interests and giving them more autonomy, power, and control over their work, which boosts their intrinsic motivation" (p. 11).

In a tech-friendly classroom, letting students choose the product they create might involve presenting two options, such as an ebook (using a tool that gives students the ability to record their voice and add text) or a web page (using a tool that gives students the ability to publish work online in the style of a blogger). Offering such choices in a digital space might feel overwhelming if your students require a significant amount of support or if you do not know all the ins and outs of various technology tools. These factors might lead you to choose a single open-ended creation tool to introduce to students at the beginning of the school year. Because an open-ended tool can be used in many different ways, you can revisit this same tool—one your students have already had experience with for a project in the beginning of the term—for different projects throughout the school year.

Setting Students Up for Success

To help students feel successful when using EdTech tools to capture their learning, you might introduce several supporting resources. Among the most common are exemplars, checklists and rubrics, and graphic organizers. All these pieces can become part of your plan for supporting students throughout the creation process.

Exemplars

An exemplar is essentially a strong example of a student project. Creating an exemplar will help both you and your students understand the direction a project should take. In addition to presenting a vision for student creators, when you create a model for student work, it will help you anticipate potential student needs and proactively determine how to address them.

Creating a model for students takes time and effort in the planning stages, but doing so can help you anticipate student questions, identify potential obstacles, and determine what technology skills are necessary for student success. If you are worried your example will be "copied" by students, your concern may signal that the task you have shared with them is too prescriptive and does not lend itself to true creative expression. In addition to sharing an example you have created, you might use past student work (with permission) or examples you have found from other educators or online sources as exemplars.

In Chapter 3, we looked at ways to generate instructional materials and supporting resources with AI. If you are struggling to find project examples to share with students, you might look for support from chatbot tools. For example, if your students will write a limerick or haiku related to a topic like world peace, you might ask a chatbot to produce examples you can share with students.

Checklists and Rubrics

Checklists and rubrics can support students as they work on any type of project. As you design tech-friendly learning opportunities for students, you might first review rubrics you have used in the past related to similar curriculum goals. For example, if your students are creating math tutorial videos, you might review the checklist or rubric you used in years past to review the explanations students wrote to share their thinking when solving a math problem, or your past expectations for how students should show their work.

Rubrics allow you to both evaluate student work and communicate expectations. Over the course of a unit, you can confer with students either formally or informally, using rubrics to guide conversations. These rubrics might include an additional row for topics unique to creating in a tech-friendly environment or addressing an audience, such as music choice in a video as it relates to the topic's tone or theme. Alternatively, you might design a checklist that connects to the digital elements of a project so students (and any peer reviewers) can make sure their creations address tech-specific elements such as sound quality, image citation, and other important considerations related to the project.

Graphic Organizers

Throughout the creation process, graphic organizers can support students as they organize their thinking and make a plan. These organizers can take a variety of forms, from a graphic organizer you have created using Google Docs to the no-tech option of a series of sticky notes. Graphic organizers might help every student in a class, but their use is not necessarily a one-size-fits-all approach. Instead, you can recommend that certain students use a particular graphic organizer based on your observations and previous data collection. For example, you might introduce a T-chart to students who you anticipate will need to categorize ideas as they work, or a vocabulary brainstorming page for another group of students before they start searching for images to add to an ebook or a slideshow.

Final Thoughts

We consume content in so many ways—all day, every day, at every age—from reading to viewing to listening to a wide range of media created by others. Our roles as consumers and creators are not mutually exclusive. Instead, as we create something new, we gain a stronger understanding of how the media we consume is developed. We become better equipped to evaluate the authority of a content creator and decide whether the source can be trusted.

Student creations can take numerous forms, and in this chapter, we have looked at essential components to consider for the work products students create. These provide a strong starting point as you consider leveraging digital tools to help students share their learning. As you dive deeper into student creations, encourage students to suggest ideas relevant to their own habits and interests as consumers of digital content. One student might decide to create a video game based on a moment in history, while another might choose to develop an app to track recycling in your community. Both need a thorough understanding of content, support with synthesizing information, and an opportunity to use technology to make and create a product expressing their learning.

In later chapters, we will examine how to give students an audience for their work and design experiences that are relevant to their interests and view of the world. First, let's look at how assessment comes into play as students consume and create tech-friendly content.

8

Assess to Check for Understanding and Pivot Instruction

evaluate, determine, estimate, judge, ascertain, learn, decide, analyze

EdTech tools can help us save time, automate repetitive tasks, and make our lives easier in many ways. Digital tools can certainly help streamline assessment tasks, but integrating technology into the way you check for understanding can also help more students show what they know and give you a more detailed picture of where they need support. Technology might help you review a stack of multiple-choice tests faster than in the past, but in this chapter, we are going beyond a Scantron machine to think about how you can best leverage the power of digital tools to elevate the entire assessment experience. If you have joined one of my webinars on formative assessment, you might have heard me say, "There is no point in collecting data you are not going to use." This chapter is all about collecting and analyzing data so you can take action through instructional pivots and interventions. We will focus on how to formatively **assess** to check for understanding before, during, and after instruction.

Digital tools provide a special benefit because they increase students' opportunities (frequency) and options (choice) to share their learning. Technology can help students quickly share their understanding of a topic and participate in a lesson. Teachers can tailor assessment routines to the unique needs of their students, who might want to jump on video to respond to a question, sketch a response to a prompt, or leverage another feature found in digital spaces to "show what they know." Digital tools can help you check for understanding, hear from every student, and make sure every learner in a classroom is on track.

Why Is This Essential?

Assessment is an essential part of every educator's work, and the use of digital tools can enhance this practice. Strong assessment routines are fundamental to figuring out what students actually need so you can make the best use of your time with them. Technology can help formative assessment become more meaningful by enabling you to collect and analyze higher-quality information from all students with greater ease and efficiency. This opens up more time for planning instructional interventions and makes it easier to integrate assessment into everyday routines for learners.

In *What Teachers Really Need to Know About Formative Assessment,* Laura Greenstein (2010) describes formative assessment as "purposefully directed toward the student. It does not emphasize how teachers deliver information but, rather, how students receive that information, how well they understand it, and how they can apply it" (p. 16). Assessment should be student-focused, and digital tools can help you adapt instruction, help students self-assess, and provide motivating experiences for students that also allow them to share their learning. Assessment is an essential component of strong instruction and requires you to consider success criteria while thinking deeply about your goals for students.

For educators, using technology to design assessments is a component of effective practice. ISTE Educator Standard Indicator 2.7.b, Use Tech to Create Assessments, states, "Use technology to design and implement a variety of formative and summative assessments that accommodate learner needs, provide timely feedback to students and inform instruction."

Formative Assessment

In *Checking for Understanding: Formative Assessment Techniques for Your Classroom,* Doug Fisher and Nancy Frey (2014) make the following suggestion:

Use these guiding questions to incorporate checking for understanding in your practice:

- Do I know what misconceptions or naïve assumptions my students possess?
- How do I know what they understand?
- What evidence will I accept for this understanding?
- How will I use their understandings to plan future instruction? (p. 14)

When technology is brought into the equation, you can build on these formative assessment foundations to dig deeper into student understanding in the following ways:

- *You can hear from more students* by using tools that let every student share, instead of hearing only those students who raise their hand.
- *You can give students more ways to respond* by using features of digital spaces, such as audio, voice-to-text, illustrations, video, and more.
- *You can better organize data* by collecting information with digital tools, ultimately saving time and energy you can reallocate to designing interventions and working directly with students.

As we look at formative assessment in a tech-rich learning environment, we can keep these best practices in mind while examining opportunities to elevate assessment routines with the help of technology. Your teaching objectives and success criteria will reflect your students' needs and your particular standards and curriculum. Let's examine strategies you can use before, during, and after instruction that will give you actionable insights to inform future learning experiences.

Before

At the beginning of a lesson or unit, you might check for understanding to see what students already know about a topic. In a tech-friendly classroom, students can post a response to a question like "What do you already know about the solar system?" in a shared space such as Padlet, FigJam, or Nearpod, where you can get a sense of how well the class understands something. Before a lesson, you might also share a more formal set of questions for students to answer with short-response options, using an app such as Microsoft Forms, Google Forms, or Socrative.

In addition to checking for understanding before kicking off a new learning experience for students, you might want to gather information on any misconceptions they might have about the topic. An activity such as a

Generating Assessment Questions with AI

A chatbot can help you generate questions to check for understanding at the beginning, middle, and end of a learning experience. Use the following prompts for inspiration, or customize them by adding in your learning objective, success criteria, or any other relevant information.

- Make a list of [number] writing prompts I can share with students in [grade level] to have them demonstrate their understanding of [topic].

  Example: Make a list of five writing prompts I can share with students in 8th grade to have them demonstrate their understanding of the causes of the American Revolution.

- Write [number] questions for a group of [grade level] to check for understanding about [topic].

  Example: Write 10 questions for a group of 2nd graders to check for understanding about the differences between weather systems.

To find more customizable prompts and blog posts related to AI, go to https://classtechtips.com/tag/ai -blog-post or scan the QR code.

Chatbot
Prompts

KWL, in which students share what they Know, Want to know, and have Learned about a topic, is a great way to gauge misconceptions. Instead of soliciting text-based responses, you might want to include options for students to record their answers in audio or video format. When students share a response to a question about a new topic, they may feel more comfortable talking about it than writing about it, regardless of their proficiency level as writers.

In my book *#FormativeTech: Meaningful, Sustainable, and Scalable Formative Assessment with Technology* (Burns, 2017), I discuss what this activity can look like in action:

> If you were collecting student poll information on an index card or sticky notes before, now you can use technology tools to make sure you've received formative assessment data from every student, right at the beginning of a lesson. Instead of *I wish I knew how much my students loved this subtopic* or *If I had known no one had read this book last year, I would have used a different example . . .* , you can now gather information efficiently and act on it in the moment. (p. 17)

Checking for understanding and looking for student misconceptions are two things to consider at the start of a lesson or unit of study. You might also introduce an activity such as a word cloud to gauge student interest in a topic. In a word cloud activity, students submit a word or two in response to a prompt such as "What else would you like to know about this topic?" Or you could create a poll or scale using a tool such as Mentimeter, Poll Everywhere, or Nearpod to have students share their comfort or confidence level about a new topic.

During

In the middle of a lesson or unit of study, you can plan to pause to check for student understanding. This can happen strategically and purposefully as part of your goal to make sure instruction is meeting students' needs. These opportunities for a midlesson pause to check for understanding should be an integral part of your plan, not an afterthought. How might this look in a tech-friendly classroom? Here are some options:

- *Turn-and-talk:* Students chat with a classmate and then submit their response to a shared space such as a discussion board (e.g., PowerSchool Schoology Learning), a collaborative board (e.g., Padlet), or a common posting area (e.g., Google Classroom).
- *Stop-and-jot:* Students pause to capture their thinking in various ways, such as drawing a picture (e.g., using Seesaw) or adding a virtual sticky note to a collaborative space (e.g., using Canvas Whiteboards).
- *Quick question:* Students respond to an open-ended short-response question so you can get a sense of their current level of understanding (e.g., using Nearpod or Pear Deck).
- *Pulse check:* Students share their confidence level, how they are feeling, or an indication of what they might need to be successful, using options such as a word cloud (e.g., Curipod), a scale (e.g., Mentimeter), or a poll (e.g., Poll Everywhere).

When planning midlesson moments to check for understanding, first determine the direction and intended outcomes of the lesson. Know where you are headed and what you would like to see students accomplish by the end of the lesson or activity. Identifying success criteria is helpful during all phases of formative assessment, including in the middle of a lesson. For example, if you poll the class and find student confidence is low, or you ask students to post responses to a question on a collaborative space and their answers raise concerns, you might decide to pivot your instruction based on their responses. Midlesson checks offer an opportunity to bring the class together for a reset. The information you collect may lead you to take immediate action, such as gathering a small group of students to review a concept, or help you know what to look out for during the remainder of the lesson.

Generative AI Tools for Assessment

Although you can generate your own prompts to enter into a chatbot space, you might find generative AI tools designed for K–12 educators worth exploring. The following are three tools that leverage this technology to support educators with their assessment goals:

- Conker: a customizable online quiz creator with multiple question types
- Curipod: an interactive lesson creator with embedded questions
- Pressto Writing Assistant: a writing prompt generator with skill and grade-level customization

After

Formative assessment is commonly used at the end of a lesson or an activity. Before students go to lunch or the bell rings, we gather information to help us make a decision about what happens the next time we meet with students. This is a crucial moment and is often where a pivot takes place, as we review data collected from students and decide what will happen next.

There are multiple ways to gather this postlesson information. Although you might pose a few multiple-choice questions to students using a tool such as Google Forms or Socrative, I would encourage you to think of how digital spaces foster opportunities for students to provide responses to open-ended questions. Such responses can take the form of a digital exit slip or an exit ticket where students are given enough time and space to share an answer to a question. You can invite students into a digital space where they have multiple options to "show what they know." Students may share in different ways (audio, video, illustration, or text), and as long as you have a clear objective for student learning and clear success criteria to help you determine students' current level of understanding, it will not matter how they decide to respond.

What should you look for when selecting digital assessment tools? There are a variety of tools that help you check for student understanding after an activity. If you want students to have options for a multimedia response, you will want to look for features like audio recording, video recording, and text responses. Although you might give students suggestions on what feature to use, your goal is not to see if they can use the technology but, rather, to determine what they know about a topic based on the question you posed. You want to give students everything they need to answer a question so you have high-quality information to work off of as you plan your future instruction.

Two examples of EdTech tools you can use for formative assessment are Flip and Seesaw. With Flip, students can post video responses to a question, draw an illustration using a whiteboard option, and add a link to something they would like to reference. Imagine you asked a group of 8th graders to identify different parts of a flower. Using Flip, one student might turn on their camera and talk about the parts of a flower while pointing to those parts on a diagram they drew. Another student might stay off camera and use the whiteboard feature to draw a picture, add labels, and record audio narration. Using a tool like Seesaw, 2nd grade students can choose how to respond to a question their teacher asks about the characteristics of different shapes. Students can respond with a drawing, a photograph, a video, or a written note, each with the option to add a caption and a voice recording. Together, all the responses could provide enough information for the teacher to get a sense of student understanding. Essentially, you want to use a tool that provides flexibility so you and your students can choose the best ways for them to respond.

Students might ask for feedback by adding a comment to a collaborative document like Google Docs. ISTE Student Standard Indicator 1.1.c, Feedback to Improve Practice, encourages students to use technology this way, stating, "Students use technology to seek feedback that informs and improves their practice and to demonstrate their learning in a variety of ways."

Using AI to Help Give Feedback to Students

As you review student work, giving timely, actionable feedback is important. If you are not sure where to start, you might ask a chatbot like ChatGPT to provide ideas for feedback that is specific to the task and expectation you have shared with students, as in the following example:

- My [grade level] students are [task/expectation], and I want to give them actionable feedback on [specific objective]. What kinds of things can I say to them to help [goal]?

Example: My 10th grade students are writing research reports on different topics related to environmental science, and I want to give them actionable feedback on their conclusions. What kinds of things can I say to them to help strengthen their writing?

The Benefits of Using Technology to Check for Understanding

In a traditional classroom setting, we know a one-size-fits-all approach is not the best option for assessment. In digital spaces, you can have students share their learning and respond to a question in different ways. For example, you might set up a journaling space for students to give responses to daily or weekly prompts. If you use a tool with audio, video, and voice-to-text options, such as Book Creator, students can pick how they respond to the prompt—and their preference of media may change throughout the week. You can determine whether a student will need additional support regardless of the technology they choose to share their response.

In *Assessment and Student Success in a Differentiated Classroom*, Carol Ann Tomlinson and Tonya R. Moon (2013) describe how "formative (ongoing) assessment lets teachers closely monitor a student's evolving knowledge, understanding, and skills—including any misunderstandings a student may have or develop about key content" (pp. 19–20). If we want actionable information, we must make sure the channels students use

Expanding the Purpose of the Exit Slip

Although we often associate sharing student work with culminating projects, we can also celebrate small moments. A multimedia response at the end of a lesson can be a cause for recognition. You might consider a dual purpose for this type of activity: (1) collecting formative assessment data and (2) giving students a chance to share their work with an audience of their peers. Graphic design tools like Adobe Express or Canva are two examples of applications students can use to create a visual that looks like the type of content they might see on social media.

In *Dive into UDL: Immersive Practices to Develop Expert Learners,* Kendra Grant and Luis Perez (2022) explore how to create more purposeful learning for students. Kendra joined me for a discussion on my (2022b) *Easy EdTech Podcast* about how to help students take more ownership of their learning (to listen, scan the QR code).

Easy EdTech Podcast: 190

to share their current understanding are adequate to capture their thinking. This is a key component of examining the value-add of technology. We can enhance students' ability to share what they know or do not yet know about a topic by increasing opportunities for them to provide an update on their current level of understanding and providing different ways for them to respond to their work. The increased frequency of student responses, the ability to review in real time, and the choice for differentiated responses may lead to higher-quality responses from students.

The way you choose to allocate time to check for understanding can vary throughout the school year. In *synchronous* (live) instruction, assessment data is gathered in the moment and often acted on immediately. In *asynchronous* (self-paced) instruction, students work at their own pace but within some kind of time constraint, such as a station rotation model during a class period or over the course of a week between one-on-one conferences or meetings. In these self-paced environments, formative assessment opportunities include regular check-ins and timely feedback. Review of student work in an asynchronous model must happen consistently, with clear action items alongside it. A student may work at their own pace over the course of a day or week, but the review of their work by a teacher can happen in a timely manner. You will want to create your own schedule for checking on student work and keep your goals related to success criteria by your side. To reflect on how you are collecting and using formative assessment data, you might ask yourself, *What do I really want students to know? What pivot or action will I take to make sure it happens?*

Taking Action with Tech-Friendly Interventions

The assessment data you collect can help you design more personalized learning pathways for students. When collecting assessment data in a traditional classroom setting, we think about gathering resources and developing interventions for students. In a digital space, we can also distribute curated resources to students based on the data we collect. This process could include creating collections of books for students within a platform such as Epic or sharing a link to a supporting tool such as the web apps from the Math Learning Center.

Taking action on formative assessment data might include a pivot in your instruction to change the series of lessons or activities you had originally planned for the whole class. This pivot provides an opportunity to reteach a strategy, review past content, or provide relevant examples to help students better understand a concept or an idea. In response to the formative assessment data you review, you might share with your students a video tutorial from Khan Academy or an explainer video from BrainPOP. Your pivots for a whole group could include posting a collection of resources in an LMS for students to examine together as a group.

After you collect formative assessment data, your action items might be specific to individual students or for small groups to address common needs. For an individual student, you might share a screencast you made with a tool like Loom or Screencastify to help them explore an idea or spotlight a helpful resource. If a few students have demonstrated a common need, you might share a link to an article with those students by posting it just for them in a common space such as Google Classroom or Microsoft Teams. In either case, digital spaces make it easy to share supplemental resources with any students who may benefit. A simple copy-and-paste of a link in an email or a message to a student in an LMS lets you quickly place a supporting resource in their hands.

Using AI to Pivot Instruction

When you review formative assessment data, you'll often find that students require a variety of supports to better understand a concept. Numerous factors can influence how you choose to differentiate a lesson. Differentiating your instruction by crafting specific interventions—or more than one version of an assignment—can be a time-consuming task. Artificial intelligence tools like ChatGPT can help you differentiate your instruction. As always, these generative AI tools only work in combination with your experience and expertise. After reviewing formative assessment data, you might find a few students need a specific intervention. You can try a prompt in a chatbot like ChatGPT, Gemini, or Claude to save you time as you act on the information you have collected and analyzed regarding the needs of your students. The following are a few examples of queries you can try to help you address the needs of just one or two students in your class or the needs of a small group:

- Explain the meaning of [word] and put it in a sentence to help a [grade level] student understand its meaning in context.
- Make a table with synonyms and antonyms for [word] in each column.
- I am teaching [topic] to [grade level]. Make a list of important vocabulary words they should know before we finish the lesson.
- Explain [topic] so it is easy for [grade level] to understand. Use a connection to [interest] to make it more engaging for them.
- Explain the process of [task] in [number] steps for [grade level] student. Use emojis or pictures to support the step-by-step guide.

Final Thoughts

When used strategically, digital tools can play an important role in your formative assessment routine and impact instructional and intervention decisions throughout a unit of study. This chapter stressed the importance of using technology to check for understanding so you can hear from all students more frequently and with more depth, increasing both quantity and quality of responses. Restructuring current formative assessment routines to incorporate EdTech tools may initially feel disruptive, but the change can provide you with higher-quality responses, more consistent check-ins, and the ability to streamline your interventions (perhaps with the support of AI) to better serve all students.

9

Share Student Creations in Big and Small Ways

---

celebrate, compliment, commend, acclaim, honor, show off

What does sharing look like in your classroom? Passing a basket of crayons or handing a tablet to a classmate definitely counts as sharing physical resources in a classroom. In this chapter, we will consider sharing in digital spaces as a way for students to show off what they have learned, talk about their experiences, and celebrate the work of their peers.

Sharing is part of our everyday lives and happens at every age. We might share an accomplishment with a friend or family member or start the day chatting with a colleague about something new we learned while listening to a podcast or reading a magazine profile. Similarly, students can share what they have learned about a topic in online spaces using features unique to digital platforms.

This chapter and the next will encompass the larger idea of setting a purpose for student work. In this chapter, we will focus on *how* students can **share** their work and *why* opportunities for sharing are so important. In the next chapter, we will examine strategies to connect student work to a relevant and authentic audience and discuss why doing so is a critical component of making student learning experiences valuable and worthwhile.

Why Is This Essential?

Learning how to share work is essential, and with so many online spaces for people of all ages to share their ideas and creations, it is more important than ever for students to know how to do so in a digital world. Although some of your students may be familiar with posting on social media, preparing them to effectively share what they know with the world goes beyond these informal exchanges. Students will need to share their ideas, obstacles, and successes through digital media, and it is essential that we prepare them to do so effectively through the use of technology.

Students of all ages should be able to (1) use speaking skills when talking about their work, (2) use listening skills when considering the work of others, and (3) share big and small artifacts of learning in digital spaces, including the incorporation of visual communications to showcase their learning with multimedia. These skills are not confined to a specific content area or age group and can apply across disciplines—as well as industries. To build students' confidence and fluency in sharing their learning in digital spaces, we can include opportunities to do so throughout the school year.

Speaking in Digital Spaces

Speaking in front of a group of peers in a classroom and answering questions next to a posterboard display as families walk around a science fair are just two examples of students sharing their work. These in-person experiences are important, and in digital spaces we ask students to accomplish the same goal, but the interaction and output are different than in a physical space. Student sharing in digital spaces might involve a live videoconference, a prerecorded video presentation, or a text-based post in a discussion space. Let's take a closer look at these three ways for students to share and speak about their work in digital spaces.

Live Videoconference

Students may share their work during a videoconference using a tool such as Zoom or Google Meet. Students can use videoconferencing to connect with partner classes, experts, or an audience that is nearby but can't physically join an event on a school campus. A videoconference can happen at a school site where students use a platform such as Microsoft

Teams or FaceTime to share their work with students in a different time zone or guest experts in another part of the world.

You may find some of your students have experience in a space like this, particularly if they took part in distance learning experiences in the early 2020s. There are a handful of skills you can help students build as they speak and share in a videoconference. These skills include how to connect to a videoconference room, how to find and look at the camera on a device when talking, how to utilize a chat space, and how to share a screen to display what is on a student device. You might decide to explore additional skills with students, such as using external microphones or cameras to improve the quality of the experiences, and even introduce logistical items like the steps needed to schedule and set up a call.

Prerecorded Video Presentation

A prerecorded video presentation is ideal for asynchronous learning opportunities or times when students want to share their work with an audience unable to attend a live event. This type of sharing is also well suited to situations in which *students* may not be able to participate in a live event or may feel more comfortable speaking about their work without the added stress of a live presentation. Prerecorded videos could consist of students speaking into the camera of a device and talking about their work or presenting a slideshow with images and narration instead of appearing on camera. Students might post a prerecorded video presentation in a common space for classmates to view as either a link or an uploaded file.

ISTE Education Leader Standard Indicator 3.1.c encourages leaders to Model Digital Citizenship with their own online interactions, stating, "Model digital citizenship by critically evaluating online resources, engaging in civil discourse online and using digital tools to contribute to positive social change." Education leaders might decide to share their own experiences with online interactions and embrace the opportunity to be role models for posting and listening in discussion spaces.

Post in a Discussion Space

Sharing in digital spaces does not require students to appear on video and talk about their work. Alternatively, you might decide to set up

Tools to Facilitate Speaking in Digital Spaces

- Google Meet: a live video-conference service that allows students to share their camera, voice, or screen as they talk about their work

- Flip: a website and mobile app where students can post prerecorded video, use a whiteboard, share their screen, and share additional links or information for an audience to engage in their work

- Clips: a mobile app where students can record short videos and access video-editing features such as the ability to add text to the screen

a space where students are encouraged to share an update (using text or a voice recording) on a project or post a link to something they are working on. In a discussion space, students can see and celebrate one another's contributions. In an elementary classroom, a tool such as Seesaw might serve as a space for students to post and share their work; it offers options to add images, links, videos, files, illustrations, and texts. You have the option to moderate student posts and turn student commenting on or off. You can also publish student work to a public blog within Seesaw to share student work with a larger audience. In a middle or high school classroom, students might share their work in a discussion space within an LMS, such as Canvas or PowerSchool Schoology Learning.

Listening in Digital Spaces

When students listen in a digital space, they should be ready to engage with the person who is sharing and prepared to celebrate that person's work. In "How to Foster Deep Listening," Kersti Tyson and colleagues (2014) examine the importance of listening and how teachers can model listening skills in any classroom. An important component of listening skills is asking what the authors call "genuine questions," which they define as "questions [that] are born of curiosity—about the topic under study or about how another person thinks about or experiences something. In the best genuine questions, the answer is unknown to the questioner" (para. 18). In a digital space—as in a physical space—you can model what strong listening skills look like by asking genuine questions, summarizing what you heard, and making connections to previous discussions.

Modeling is only part of the process of helping students strengthen their listening skills. Providing time and opportunities for listening—to practice these skills—is also important. In "More Than Words: Developing Core Speaking and Listening Skills," Jessica Roake and Laura Varlas (2013) discuss the value of "creating a space in which students feel safe and empowered in sharing their ideas." In a digital environment, a safe space is one where students have time to put their growing listening skills into practice and build the confidence to engage in conversations with classmates. They need time to try to engage in the thoughtful back-and-forth of listening, questioning, and responding—a skill needed in all subject areas, at all ages. Creating such a space might include allocating time for students to share their learning with peers on a more regular basis instead of only at the end of a unit of study.

Sharing Big and Small, Throughout the School Year

There is no need to hold off on sharing and celebrating student work until the end of a unit or the last few days of a multiweek project. Instead, consider increasing the frequency with which students share, even including a sharing component at the end of each lesson. Doing so sets a purpose for students as they work each day and adds a layer of accountability and celebration to everyday activities. Incorporating these opportunities to share can address myriad goals. Let's first examine activities for everyday sharing in tech-friendly spaces, before moving on to sharing as a culminating activity.

Everyday Sharing

Students can share their work as part of a routine you use at the end of every lesson or a few times a week. Carving out time for everyday sharing can coincide with your goals for community building, engagement, and accountability. The moments when students share might also serve as formative assessment opportunities to guide future instruction.

In an early-elementary classroom, students can record a video in which they share an illustration they created and point to the picture as they talk about what they drew. They can post this to a collaborative space such as Seesaw for their classmates and family members to see.

In an upper-elementary classroom, students might use Flip or Clips to create a video about a book they are reading and add emojis or stickers to their screen to represent how they feel about the book so far. Students can share this update at the end of a literacy block if they are working together in the classroom or share it in a common digital space like an LMS if they are working asynchronously, such as in a station rotation model.

In a middle school classroom, students might create a digital exit ticket in response to a prompt by making a photo collage and adding text to their graphic. They can use a tool such as Canvas or Adobe Express to make the graphic. Students can share it in a discussion space set up by their teacher, such as Padlet, alongside a text or audio explanation for their classmates to see.

In a high school classroom, students might show a partner what they added to a presentation they are working on, including new images or text they added to a slide deck. After sharing with their classmates, they can post a link to the updates they made as a way to share and celebrate the process, in addition to a final product.

Over the course of the school year, students may become familiar with multiple ways to share their learning. ISTE Student Standard Indicator 1.6.a, Choose Platforms or Tools, encourages students to take agency in the sharing process. It states, "Students choose the appropriate platforms and tools for meeting the desired objectives of their creation or communication."

Sharing as a Culminating Activity

When we think of sharing student work, culminating projects are usually the first thing that comes to mind. An end-of-unit project, a multi-day activity, or a project that students work on for several weeks would fall into this category.

This type of sharing and celebration can take many forms and include an opportunity to extend the sharing of student work beyond the classroom walls and include community members. In addition to having an in-person event where family and schoolmates gather with your class, you might create a virtual space for sharing. A virtual space could include a class blog, a livestream event, or a collaborative product like an ebook compilation of student work posted on a school or district website. The following examples show various ways students and teachers can leverage digital tools to share culminating projects.

In an early-elementary classroom, students might create a video featuring a place in the community they want to visit. The teacher can post the videos on a class website created with a website builder like Google Sites and share the link to the page with families.

In an upper-elementary classroom, students might use an open-ended creation tool like Book Creator to publish an ebook of poetry they have written about the seasons of the year. They can display their poetry anthologies on the screens of their Chromebooks, and families or a partner class can visit and walk around the room to see what everyone has made.

In a middle school classroom, students might use a tool such as the web page builder in Adobe Express or Microsoft Sway to create a landing page (a web page where users "land" after clicking on a link) showcasing all the pictures they snapped during a science experiment. On this landing page, they can include additional information such as their future research plans. Students can share the link to the landing page in the chat space of a videoconference in which they talk about their experiment with a subject-matter expert or with family members who participate in the livestream event.

In a high school classroom, you might create a podcast with your class using a combination of tools, like QuickTime and GarageBand, in which pairs of students each record and edit one episode featuring an interview with an industry expert. You or a group of students can upload the episodes to a common space such as a shared folder where their classmates will be able to locate and listen to the other episodes in the class-created podcast.

Sharing in Public Spaces

Sharing student work in public spaces can fall into two categories—local and global—each with plenty of ways to customize the experience. Sharing locally might include a class celebration, schoolwide assemblies, Family Night exhibits, or presentations to the school board. Each of these involves a closed group of audience members based in your school or district who will consume and celebrate the work students have shared. Sharing globally might include connecting with a partner class in another time zone, publishing links to student creations on school or district social media pages, or publishing students' work with a public link online so they can easily share their work with extended family members. Each type of sharing has benefits, but one critical consideration is student privacy and the need to secure permission from both families and students.

Sharing should be encouraged but not forced. Even if students technically have permission from their families to post their work online, students should consent to this as well. Just as you might ask students if they feel comfortable standing in front of the class or ask them if they would like to share something they have written or worked on before calling on them, it is important for students to understand that they have agency and a voice when their work is shared with the world. You might ask students questions such as these:

- We have permission to share our ebooks on the school website. Is it OK if I include yours to show off what a great job you did with this project?
- Can we share your accomplishment with our school community by posting a picture of your work on the school Instagram account?

Securing permission is a consideration for all students—from kindergartners to high schoolers.

Student Branding

Digital Storytelling

The term *digital storytelling* is often associated with narrative writing in which students use technology to tell real or imagined stories. A broader definition applies when placing this term in the context of this chapter. When students tell the story of their learning and share it with their peers and others, their work extends beyond a single screen to become available to a wider audience. Author and fellow Apple Distinguished Educator Michael Hernandez joined me on my (2023f) *Easy EdTech Podcast* to discuss digital storytelling, the topic of his 2024 ISTE book *Storytelling with Purpose,* and the idea of "uncheatable assessments" as it relates to creativity in the classroom. Listen to the full conversation by scanning the QR code.

Easy EdTech Podcast: 214

The idea of online branding might seem to apply only to Instagram influencers or entrepreneurs. But branding is really all about sharing intentionally. *Entrepreneur* magazine defines *branding* as "the marketing practice of creating a name, symbol, or design that identifies and differentiates a product from other products" (*Entrepreneur,* n.d.). You might introduce this concept to students by having them think about the type of messaging they want to get across, using discussion questions such as these:

- How do you want people to feel when they see your work?
- What colors do you love?
- If you had a logo, what would it look like?
- How would you describe yourself using only one sentence?

Conversations on branding may seem like a natural fit in a high school classroom, but even early-elementary school students can provide answers to these questions.

To help students explore the concept of a brand, you might ask them to think of a company they regularly interact with and the words they would use to describe it. This is a concept that may initially require clear modeling. For example, you might say, "When I think of [company] and enter their store, it makes me feel [emotion]. I would describe them with these three [adjectives]."

Students can begin to think about the types of fonts they like to use and their favorite color palettes and even design a logo to accompany their creations throughout the school year. Creating a logo is also a great way to introduce a graphic design tool you might revisit for several student projects over the course of the school year.

Final Thoughts

Learning how to share work in digital spaces is essential. From communicating with visuals to building speaking and listening skills, students need to experience how to share their work online. By providing a digital space for students to share, we can elevate their voices and celebrate their accomplishments (big and small) throughout the school year. An emphasis on sharing the *process* in addition to the final *product* is a great way to emphasize the importance of the learning journey. It is also a good way to help students see how generative AI applications—which often seem like a "quick win" for creating something like an essay with little effort—are only one tool in our digital tool belts and not a replacement for the creative process. In the next chapter, we will build on the idea of sharing student work by connecting it to an audience. The combination of *knowing how* to share their learning with *opportunities* to share their learning can help students see their work as purposeful and authentic.

10

Connect Students to Authentic Audiences

join, link up, unify, convene, gather, league, fuse

Buzzing classrooms where students are hard at work often have at least one thing in common: students have a specific goal. They know where they are going and what needs to be done to get there. This observation is as true in a 1st grade classroom where you might see students designing covers for narrative stories they have written to share with families as it is in an 8th grade classroom where you could find students creating posters with public service announcements to share with a local community center.

There are many factors to consider when planning a lesson or an activity for students, from designing scaffolds and supports to incorporating formative assessment. Setting a clear intention for classroom learning experiences and communicating that purpose to students is crucial. One way to set a purpose or an intention for students is to connect their learning experiences—and the work they create—to a relevant and authentic audience. In other chapters, we have explored student creations (Chapter 7) and ways for students to share their work with their school community and the larger world (Chapter 9). This chapter is about setting an *intention* for sharing student learning—to **connect** students with an audience and set a purpose for their learning.

Why Is This Essential?

When work is relevant to students, they understand *why* they are doing something and see it as a valuable use of their time. Relevant work has meaning for students and relates to their interests and current circumstances. In *The Relevant Classroom: 6 Steps to Foster Real-World Learning,* Eric Hardie (2019) discusses the importance of making sure the content students are working with is relevant and authentic. Hardie states, "Every single school has the resources required—they just need to start *really* listening to their students and letting them take the lead" (p. 15). Part of making content relevant is linking it to an audience. Number four on Hardie's list of six steps is "connect student work to the community," and he emphasizes the need to provide an audience for students.

Connecting student work to an audience is perhaps more important than ever, as online sharing prevails in our digital world. Most students are familiar with what it means to have content shared online, and some may even be aspiring content creators. Here is how the digital marketing company HubSpot defines *content creator:*

> A content creator produces entertaining or educational material that caters to the interests and challenges of a target audience. The content he/she produces can take many forms, including blog posts, videos, e-books, photos, and infographics. Today, businesses employ content creators to engage new and existing customers on the brand's behalf. (Butler, n.d., para. 5)

Students who consume online media can probably name some of their favorite content creators. For high school students, this might include a favorite podcaster or TikToker, and elementary school students might be able to name a few different YouTube channels.

This chapter is not about how to turn your students into social media influencers—far from it. However, in today's online world, students are well positioned to identify creators of content and observe how they connect with their audience. Students expect their own creations to be viewed and celebrated, and having an authentic audience is critical. In *The Motivated Student: Unlocking the Enthusiasm for Learning,* Bob Sullo (2009) describes how "[we] are born with powerful basic needs," and he places the need "to connect with others" at the start of the list (p. 48). We must understand how to address this need with students in a digital world. Technology tools can help facilitate and foster connections to authentic and relevant audiences.

Beginning with the Audience in Mind

For students to find an experience truly relevant, they need to relate to the topic in some way. Students should be able to identify why learning about this topic is important not only in a classroom setting but also in the context of the larger world. In *The Purposeful Classroom: How to Structure Lessons with Learning Goals in Mind,* Douglas Fisher and Nancy Frey (2011) state, "The *purpose* has to be understood by students such that they can explain it in their own words and grasp its relevance" (p. 6). When planning a learning experience for students, you can begin with the end in mind and identify an audience for their work.

ISTE Educator Standard Indicator 2.5.b, Design Authentic Learning Activities, stresses the importance of having an audience for student creations. It states, "Design authentic learning activities that align with content area standards and use digital tools and resources to maximize active, deep learning."

In an elementary classroom, you might kick off a unit on marine ecosystems by introducing the project your students will complete later in the month. You can share the website of an aquarium that might be too far away for a field trip but has a marine biologist on staff who will be part of a videoconference with your class. At the start of the unit, you can share with students how this expert will join in a virtual Zoom class celebration of the ebooks they create as part of their animal research projects.

In a middle school classroom, you might start a unit on geometry by sharing information about a podcast project students will work on during the unit. You can describe how pairs of students will each create a five-minute episode for a class podcast in which they talk about an unexpected way geometry affects their daily lives. At the beginning of the unit, you can connect students with a partner class studying the same topic but located in a different state or country. The distant class can also participate in a podcast project, and students can swap their episodes to listen to one another's creations.

In a high school classroom, you might begin a unit on civic engagement by introducing a video project students will complete over the next several weeks. You can share a few examples of 30-second video clips designed to encourage community members to vote in an upcoming election. Students can make short clips or vertical videos (similar to TikTok videos or Instagram Reels) to play on a loop on a digital screen outside a community center.

In the next chapter, we will examine transferable skills and their connection to computational thinking and computer science. If you are focusing on computer science or coding topics in your classroom, you might have students create an application to solve a problem in your school or local community. From tracking recycling in the school lunchroom to monitoring traffic patterns at an intersection in your town, there are many uses for apps students can build with a clear intention and connection to a local audience.

Social Justice and Taking Action

For an audience to be relevant to students, it should have meaning in their lives. To ensure this is the case, you can develop opportunities for students to create learning products connected to issues of social justice. Although your curriculum may not explicitly cover social justice issues, you may decide to incorporate action taking as part of a commitment to creating relevant and authentic learning experiences for students, or to connect to social and emotional learning goals as discussed in Chapter 5.

In an elementary classroom, students might read books celebrating diversity or explore issues related to biases. They can choose one book to spotlight and create a video book trailer to introduce the book to students in another class. You might have students connect these videos to a QR code, print the QR code on sticker paper, and add it to an interactive bulletin board in the school library.

Using Generative AI to Brainstorm Potential Audiences

Locating and introducing an audience for a student project can feel like an intimidating task. Whether you are new to this concept or simply looking for fresh ideas, you may find more success using a chatbot to brainstorm than conducting a Google search. The following are a few prompts you can try in a tool like ChatGPT or Gemini to brainstorm potential audiences to connect students with:

- My students are working on [topic] and will create [project]. What types of subject-matter experts could serve as an audience for their work?

- I want to design an engaging project to help [grade level] students learn about [topic]. Provide a list of ideas that include an audience for their work.

- I'm looking for an unexpected way to share the [project] my students have completed. We already plan on sharing the projects with [audience]. What other types of audiences can I connect students with?

In a middle school classroom, students might interview members of their community to give the interviewees an opportunity to share their life experiences. For example, you might have students ask a question such as "What is something about your life that would surprise others?" or "What was your biggest challenge when you were my age?" These questions could also connect to a community member's experience during a specific period in history. Students can record these interviews for a podcast shared on a public feed and promoted on a school or district website, or connect to an institution like a local historical society as another audience for their creations.

Social Justice Resources

The Southern Poverty Law Center created Learning for Justice as a free resource of supplemental materials to support social justice topics and anti-bias education and encourage students to challenge prejudice. If you are looking for support in designing learning experiences related to these issues and connecting students to an audience, you can learn more at www.learningforjustice.org.

In a high school classroom, students might read a selection of news articles and choose a social justice topic to learn more about with further research. Students can create a slideshow or photo essay with images they have taken themselves or curated from online sources. Their presentation can include links to websites where a viewer can learn more about the topic. Although students might share their presentations with classmates, you can help them expand this audience by connecting them with an organization with a similar passion for the topic they chose to spotlight.

Author's Purpose: Persuade, Entertain, Inform

A reader should be able to identify why an author wrote a particular piece. We commonly refer to this as an *author's purpose*. An English language arts teacher may have experience introducing different types of writing to students and exploring the purpose of an author who is creating text for someone to read.

ISTE Student Standard Indicator 1.6.d, Customize the Message, stresses the importance of understanding your intention for sharing with an audience. It states, "Students publish or present content that customizes the message and medium for their intended audiences."

Three core purposes are to persuade, to entertain, and to inform a reader. Although there are variations and nuances to these three overarching categories, understanding them can help in developing learning experiences that ask students to connect to a relevant and authentic audience.

Products in the *persuade* category seek to change or influence the opinion of the viewer, reader, or listener. A public service announcement, an editorial, a commercial, or an advertisement would fall into this category. The audience for this type of student product should be an individual or a group of people who are invested in the issue, are affected by the topic, and are open to changing their mind. So if students create a persuasive piece, their audience should be a group that could actually be persuaded by their argument. The following are a few examples of persuasive products in different subject areas and grade levels:

- *Early-elementary ELA:* a video to convince classmates to read a favorite book, pointing to favorite parts (filmed with Flip)
- *Upper-elementary social studies:* a letter to the principal of the school about a pressing issue, like homework policies (written with Google Docs)
- *Middle school math:* a video detailing the steps to solve a problem using one particular algorithm, making a case for why this algorithm is a better choice than other options (made with Explain Everything)
- *High school science:* a podcast episode in which two students debate a topic, trying to convince listeners to agree with them (recorded with Soundtrap)

A student creation designed to *entertain* an audience provides value to a group while students apply skills related to the academic goals for that unit or activity. Such creations might include creative writing projects or multimedia presentations. Students might make a short video where they re-create a notable moment in history or compose a song inspired by a novel. This type of student product often elicits an emotional response from an audience, such as laughter or tears. The following are a few examples:

- *Early-elementary science:* a poem about students' favorite season, including an illustration (written with Seesaw)
- *Upper-elementary math:* a comic strip with two characters trying to solve a tricky math problem, include captions and dialogue (created with Storyboard That)
- *Middle school social studies:* a skit detailing a day in the life of a notable person in history, including music (written and filmed with iMovie)

- *High school ELA:* a song to accompany a piece of creative writing, including instruments that connect to the tone (composed with GarageBand)

Student work products designed to *inform* an audience about a topic may include explanations or tutorials. In digital spaces, students can create infographics, interactive presentations, and summaries of their learning in a variety of contexts. Establishing a clear audience can help guide students during the production process, particularly in choosing a media format appropriate for this specific group. To find exemplars for this type of project, you might share an explainer video from TED-Ed or an article from Newsela. The following are a few product examples for this category:

- *Early-elementary social studies:* a class book about a day in the life of a person in the community, including audio and text (written with Book Creator)
- *Upper-elementary ELA:* a website to share research on a high-interest topic, including citations (designed with Adobe Express)
- *Middle school science:* an infographic with facts about an animal and its habitat, including data points and icons (made with Canva)
- *High school math:* a step-by-step guide with tips for solving a particular type of math problem, including images or examples (created with Google Slides)

Creating an Audience for Everyday Learning

In Chapter 9, we examined everyday activities that let students share their work, including culminating projects at the end of a unit. Who are the audiences for learning that takes place throughout a unit of study, or the "everyday" moments we know are worthy of celebration? Classmates and families are built-in audiences for everyday learning, but they are not the only ones who can support students and review their work when smaller learning activities are ready to share.

Finding an audience for everyday learning might include posting a compilation of student work on a social media feed and tagging an organization interested in the topic. For example, are students studying national symbols? You can post student exit tickets with facts they learned about the Statue of Liberty on an Instagram post and tag the account @StatueEllisNPS to connect with the National Park Service at the Statue of Liberty National Monument & Ellis Island Museum of Immigration. Another option is to invite an expert on a topic to a class video meeting where students can share questions they have prepared. Alternatively, you might contact a subject-matter expert and give them access to student submissions in a digital space such as Flip. They can watch the short videos students post and record a quick response of their own. As a reminder, posting student work and images or videos of students in online spaces accessible outside your classroom will require permission.

Creating Real Audiences for Student Work

Educational technology specialist Jennifer Hall joined me on my (2022a) *Easy EdTech Podcast* to talk about ways for students to share their creations with an authentic audience. To listen to the conversation and hear Jennifer's classroom stories, scan the QR code.

Easy EdTech Podcast: 165

Making It Relevant

In addition to identifying high-interest topics and connecting students to a specific audience for their work, you can make learning experiences more relevant by encouraging students to draw inspiration from the products they consume. We looked at students as navigators and consumers of online spaces in the first two chapters of this book. When students create content that mirrors what they consume online, their creations can feel more relevant as you connect to their own experiences navigating digital spaces.

What does this approach look like in action? You can embrace the features of popular media for creators—such as short videos made for TikTok or Instagram Reels—without ever opening an app or having a deep discussion about the platform. For example, you might ask students to create a quick step-by-step guide for lab safety in the same fast-paced format of the 30- or 45-second tutorial videos popular on social media. Or you might ask students to share facts about a historic period and have each fact pop up on the screen to the beat of a popular song. If you are not a consumer of the same media students regularly interact with, you might search popular hashtags on those platforms to find inspiration. Alternatively, you can open the floor to students. Particularly at the secondary level, you can hear from students about how they would like to connect the same content-creation strategies they consume to a project in your class. And, of course, it is important to share examples of these types of products and not assume all students have the same media consumption habits.

Although early-elementary students may not consume viral content on social media, they have likely seen music videos, videos of read-aloud books, and presentations of other educational content in multimedia formats both inside the classroom and at home. As previously mentioned, a good way to make content creation opportunities relevant to students is to mirror the type of content they consume. For example, if your elementary students are accustomed to watching videos of books being read aloud by authors, they might create a similar type of video. They can point out parts of the book or talk about details in an illustration, just like the authors in the videos they are used to watching themselves.

Final Thoughts

Connecting students to an audience is an intentional act that sets a purpose for learning and leads students to view their work as authentic and meaningful. Students who participate in relevant learning experiences see the value of applying their time to a classroom task. Identifying an audience for students and connecting them to this audience can promote accountability and set a destination for learning in your classroom. And if you are struggling to identify the perfect audience for student creations, generative AI tools like chatbots can help you brainstorm ideas. At the start of a new learning experience—big or small—you can set the intention of sharing student work with the larger world.

11

Transfer Skills Across Digital Spaces

shift, move, relocate, reassign, hand over, redistribute

One of the exciting and challenging aspects of working with educational technology is the changing nature of digital spaces. New technology may come our way at any time, with new buttons to press and new ways to think about interacting online. This reality is not a reason to throw our hands in the air and abandon all hope. Instead, it provides an important—an *essential*—issue to tackle. With new technology entering the scene, including artificial intelligence tools, *transferable skills are essential* now more than ever.

The saying "We don't know what we don't know" came up earlier in this book, and it is relevant here as well. Chapter 5 was all about exploring virtual spaces and asking questions to learn about the world. In this chapter, we will consider how students can build the independence and autonomy they need to problem-solve on their own and to ask for help when they need it. Part of this effort is helping students think logically, make predictions, and take their knowledge of one thing and apply it to a related experience.

Students need to build skills they can **transfer** across digital platforms to prepare them to successfully tackle and embrace any new developments in technology—including ones that seem like just a dream at the moment. The widespread adoption of AI-powered tools and the incorporation of generative artificial intelligence into our workflows only reinforces the need for all of us, including students, to feel confident and capable enough to adapt to a changing technological landscape. In this chapter, we'll explore strategies that can help students build transferable skills to set them up for success when a new platform, product, or digital experience (like AI) comes their way.

Why Is This Essential?

When you help students develop a transferable skill set, you prepare them to tackle situations they have not yet encountered. Students who are independent and adaptable, understand when and how to troubleshoot, and can identify the logic and patterns in digital spaces will have a skill set they can apply in many different situations. The goal of developing transferable skills is to prepare students to interact in both current and future online spaces, even if we do not yet know what those spaces will look like.

In *Teaching Students to Drive Their Brains,* Donna Wilson and Marcus Conyers (2016) say this about students:

> Wherever their ambitions lead them, they will benefit from becoming creative problem solvers, analytical thinkers, and effective communicators and collaborators. . . . Some of the most vital and versatile skillsets we can teach students to develop are the abilities to think about their learning; to be aware of factors that affect their intellectual performance; to know how, when, where, and why to use particular cognitive strategies; and to monitor and adjust their performance of learning tasks. (p. 1)

Building Independence and Autonomy

A popular phrase in elementary classrooms is "Ask three before me." This statement encourages students to approach three classmates with any question they have *before* asking their teacher. Building independence is an important practice at every grade level, in all subject areas, with or without digital tools. You might have used a routine like this one with your students or developed another structure or set of expectations to help students work independently.

As you think about how to build independent learners, you may make connections to a practice such as a Socratic seminar. In the moment, it can feel easier to give students the answer to a question they have, but instead of choosing this short-term solution, you can respond to students with follow-up questions to help them move through the stages of finding an answer on their own. Although doing so requires more patience and time, there are long-term benefits. As students navigate digital spaces, you can prompt them with questions that lead to the next step toward finding their answer. The following are examples of questions to help guide students to an answer to their question and build their independence:

- Why do you think this might have happened?
- What is another strategy or approach we could try?
- If we're not sure what to do, where can we go to find help?
- Let's search for help. What terms will we need to use if we look online for an answer?
- Is there a discussion forum or support group that can help us?
- Who might be able to help us find a solution?
- If we want to use a chatbot for help, what prompt could help us find a solution?

Independent Study

The term *independent study* might resonate with you if you ever had to earn a few extra college credits to finish a program or had a specific interest but could not find a course on the topic at your high school or university. An independent study provides an opportunity for students to explore a topic that they are interested in but might not be offered as a traditional course. It also provides a chance for students to build transferable skills as they navigate technology connected to a high-interest topic.

Of course, this type of project is different from one in which all students might participate during the school year. For example, a student participating in an independent study might create a slideshow to show the steps they took for their individual science experiment. An independent study is self-directed, and students might decide they want to use digital tools outside your realm of expertise.

What might this look like in a middle or high school classroom? You might have a student who wants to build a website to showcase their sketches for a fashion line, or a student who wants to build 3D models for car parts they have designed. If you do not have expertise in building websites or creating 3D models, your support for students will not include sharing tips for using CAD (computer-aided design) software or instruction in HTML coding. Instead, your support will be around strategies students can use to learn a new skill online. You can show them how to find and vet online courses, how to search YouTube for highly rated or recently posted videos, and how to use support forums or search queries to find answers to common or specific questions.

Despite the flexibility that comes with working on one's own, independent study programs can still have structure and clear expectations for students. Students who work on independent tasks can take part in peer and teacher feedback and benefit from opportunities to convene in groups of their peers to explore more general topics (such as project management and time management) with applications to their specific areas of study.

If you work with students who need more support, including elementary school students, you might incorporate some independent-study principles into the task development for your group. For example, you might give students more choice in the types of tools they use to create a culminating project. Or you might share step-by-step guides to take them through the process of navigating a new tool on their own. In an elementary classroom, you want to find the balance between offering support and encouraging students to solve problems independently. Every student is different, and you will want to make sure students are not frustrated or overwhelmed as you encourage them to find answers to their questions or work at their own pace.

A variety of resources can support elementary school students as they build independence. You might share anchor charts with screenshots from tools you use regularly as a class or post guides students can reference when they need help navigating a particular online space. For example, if your 1st grade students typically use Seesaw to capture their learning at the end of a math lesson, you can create a visual, such as an anchor chart displaying the steps they must take to submit their work. When students forget what to do, instead of directly telling them which button to press, refer to the chart when you respond. You can point to the steps that go along with each visual so they will become increasingly independent each time they consult the anchor chart and can begin to understand how to use reference materials to support their independence.

Modeling Problem Solving

In Chapter 1, we looked at how modeling our own online searches can help students understand how to navigate online spaces. We can model how to find a solution to a problem in the same way we might model how to use a logic strategy in an algebra class or how to find the meaning of a new word in an English language arts classroom. This practice can help students build and strengthen skills related to tech independence and problem solving.

A great way to incorporate this into your practice is to think aloud in a moment when something "goes wrong." For example, if the wireless connection stops working or a program is not loading the way it should, you can troubleshoot and create a teachable moment for students at the same time. Alternatively, if something unexpected happens, you might ask students to share what they might do in the same situation and follow their steps. You can try this even if you *do* know how to solve the problem.

These teachable moments will not be the only times you model problem solving for students. Just as you might think aloud as you demonstrate how to move through the steps of a science experiment you conduct with a class of 4th graders, you can intentionally plan to model smaller problem-solving moments in your classroom. Here are some examples of such moments:

- When you want to find the answer to a question such as "Who is the author of this book?" or "What year did this battle take place?" show how you go to Google and type in keywords to conduct a search and then choose a response on the list from a trustworthy publication or organization.
- When you want to find another way to explain a strategy, show how you go to YouTube and try a few different search terms to find a helpful video.
- When you struggle to explain something concisely, show how you can open a chatbot like ChatGPT to have it break down a big idea or concept into simpler language.
- When you are not sure how to find the button to complete a task, show how you might look for it by talking about what you have seen in other tools, such as, "I know the Save button is usually somewhere near the menu," or "I use the shortcut Control-C to copy something when I am working in Google Docs, so maybe that will work here, too."

Thinking Like a Developer

CareerExplorer (n.d.) defines an app developer as a "developer who specializes in creating mobile applications . . . with a team of designers, project managers, and other developers to create an app that meets the needs of its intended audience. This includes understanding the requirements of the app, designing the user interface and user experience, developing the app's functionality, and testing the app to ensure that it works properly" (paras. 1, 2). When students think like a developer, they go beyond the experience of simply being a participant and put themselves in the shoes of the creator of an experience. In the same way students can become smarter consumers when they take on the role of creator, when students think like a developer, they apply transferable skills. The goal is to get students thinking about design and navigational decisions, so they can navigate effectively and predict what an online experience will look like based on their previous experience in other digital spaces.

When students put on their "developer hats," they can have conversations about their experience using a tool. Here are a few examples of questions you can tailor to different groups of students as you encourage them to think like a developer:

- Why is this button in the upper-right corner of the screen?
- How does this remind you of other tools?
- Where should I go if I need help?
- How is the menu on this site organized?
- Why did the developer decide to include this feature?

One way to help students think like developers is to have them create something of their own. Although creating an app or coding a website might not be the exact task you bring into your classroom, you might decide to have students "think like their audience" when they create products of any type. In Chapter 10, we discussed the importance of connecting student work to a relevant and authentic audience. Doing so

Teaching Tech Fluency in Early Childhood Classrooms

In episode 82 of my (2020b) *Easy EdTech Podcast*, early childhood educator Pana Asavavatana shares strategies for using technology with young students. Pana discusses how she teaches tech fluency with icons using some of her favorite tools, including Seesaw and Book Creator. To listen, scan the QR code.

Easy EdTech Podcast: 82

More recently, in episode 224 (2023b), Debbie Tannenbaum expands on this idea with strategies for introducing icons to elementary school students. To listen, scan the QR code.

Easy EdTech Podcast: 224

gives them purpose and illustrates how classroom concepts apply to the world outside school. Determining the needs of an audience is an important part of the creative process and something to include in discussions with student creators. For example, students might "think like their audience" when choosing music for a book trailer, knowing music can help an audience understand the mood and themes of a book. You might also have students reflect on their own user experience using different digital tools when they discuss the experience they want to create for someone who visits their online portfolio or reads an ebook they have created.

Learning How to Troubleshoot

Although I have never sent this link to a friend or family member, I always laugh when I think about the website LetMeGoogleThat.com. The premise of the website is that there are people in our lives (including ourselves) who will ask a question they could have answered with a Google search. We want students to have the independence to know there are places where they can find answers to questions they have about using digital tools both with and without our support. Here are some questions you can suggest students ask themselves to support their troubleshooting efforts:

- What have I done in the past when encountering similar problems?
- Have I tried a "simple solution" first, such as restarting my computer or refreshing the web page?
- What are two things I can do next, and which one will I try first?
- Do I have a friend who knows a little bit more about this than I do? Can I ask them for help?
- Is there an expert who knows a lot more about this than I do? Do they have a YouTube channel or website with the answer?

So much of troubleshooting involves creative thinking skills and applying what we have learned in one environment to a new space. This process is the essence of developing the transferable skills we want students to master as they switch from one digital platform to another.

Questions for Reflection and Planning

- How often do I give students the answer to their questions about how to navigate a tool or find a solution to a problem?
- Do I give students a chance to troubleshoot before offering support or guidance?
- Do students feel comfortable asking a friend a question or using a supporting resource like Google or YouTube?
- Have I added "think aloud" moments to my plan for today's lesson?
- Do I take advantage of teachable moments when they occur in my classroom?
- Instead of offering a solution, what kinds of questions can I ask to lead students to an answer?

Learning How to Be Adaptable

Students with transferable skills are adaptable when moving from one online space to the next. If they open a program they have used every day for a year and see it has had a major update overnight, they know how to leverage their past experiences. When students open a brand-new tool for the first time, they can use what they have learned from navigating other spaces and apply it to their new digital experience.

The following prompts include the type of language you might use when modeling for students how to be adaptable in a new space:

- This must be how . . .
- This reminds me of . . .
- This must be where . . .
- This is similar to . . .
- I bet this button means . . .
- I have seen something like this before . . .
- I wonder if this button . . .
- I have never seen this before, but I bet . . .

In addition to modeling with these sentence starters, look out for the language students use as they navigate new spaces. You can identify how they make connections to past experiences and validate those strategies in your one-on-one conversations and whole-class discussions. You might say, "I noticed how you . . ." or "I was excited to see you remembered how this connects to . . .".

Computational Thinking Without Computers

ISTE CT Competencies

To review the ISTE Computational Thinking Competencies, go to https://iste.org/standards/computational-thinking-competencies or scan the QR code.

ISTE CT
Competencies

Computational thinking does not need to include computers—at least not exclusively. On the surface, this statement might seem like a crazy thing to say, especially for those who are not familiar with computer science. As we discuss how to help students build transferable skills, there are clear connections to computational thinking.

Let's start with patterns. In an early-elementary classroom, the concept of patterns is a big part of mathematical and literacy foundations. Students at this level look for patterns as they count to 100 and identify patterns in the way words are spelled.

Patterns apply in science as well, as elementary school students learn about the seasons. They take what they know to be true about one thing and apply it to other situations to see if the same rule applies. This approach is a foundational concept of computational thinking and is an example of transferable skills in action.

ISTE Student Standard 1.5 describes a computational thinker as follows: "Students develop and employ strategies for understanding and solving problems in ways that leverage the power of technological methods to develop and test solutions." ISTE Student Standard Indicator 1.5.c, Decompose Problems, states, "Students break problems into component parts, extract key information and develop descriptive models to understand complex systems or facilitate problem-solving."

Computational Thinking in Every Subject

As you explore problem-solving strategies and the role of computational thinking in your classroom, you may want to check out my conversation with ISTE author Jorge Valenzuela on my (2020a) *Easy EdTech Podcast.* Jorge, the author of *Rev Up Robotics* (2020), shares how to use the foundations of computational thinking in any subject area. Listen to the full episode by scanning the QR code.

Easy EdTech Podcast: 66

Many elementary topics include a connection to patterns, and the skills come into play in middle and high school classrooms as well. Students look for patterns and apply algorithms as they solve a math problem; they search for patterns in a biology classroom as they examine marine wildlife or learn about rock cycles. Part of helping students build transferable skills is understanding how to identify components of instruction related to computational thinking.

ISTE Student Standard Indicator 1.5.d, Algorithmic Thinking, relates to the concept of working with and without digital tools. It states, "Students understand how automation works and use algorithmic thinking to develop a sequence of steps to create and test automated solutions."

To use skills in multiple contexts, students must enter new situations with an *asset mindset,* feeling confident in what they already know and viewing their current knowledge as a foundation to build upon. Your school might already have an established program for computer science

**Making Connections
with the Help of a Chatbot**

Teaching computational thinking and computer science standards may feel intimidating for educators who do not have a lot of experience with these topics. One way to help is to ask a chatbot to make connections between what you are already teaching and a skill or concept that falls into this category. You can customize and try the following prompt inside a tool like ChatGPT: "Help me see the connection between computer science skills like [specific example] and [what I'm teaching this week]."

or decide to introduce instruction in computer science skills into the school day. Even if you do not have a dedicated computer science program, these ideas can fit into the work your students do every day, at all ages, in every subject area.

Final Thoughts

With artificial intelligence, particularly generative AI, front of mind for so many educators, we can connect the skills students and educators already have to these evolving spaces. From understanding how to conduct an online search to evaluating sources, students and educators can transfer the skills they've developed in the last decade to the newer generative AI platforms that require these foundational skills. It is essential for students to develop transferable skills they can apply to a variety of digital environments. When students step back and think about their interactions with specific EdTech tools, encourage them to notice similarities and differences across devices and platforms and practice problem solving and critical thinking in authentic digital spaces. These experiences can build independence and ensure students are prepared to transfer the skill they develop in one space to multiple digital spaces. The development of transferable skills ensures students are prepared for an ever-changing and evolving digital landscape.

12

Plan for Tech-Rich Learning Experiences

arrange, strategize, design, program, map, organize, prepare

Over the preceding 11 chapters, we have examined essential EdTech concepts to ensure we are making the most of digital tools for teaching and learning. This final chapter centers on planning—specifically, planning for a variety of instructional models both inside and outside the classroom. In this chapter, we will look at how to **plan** for tech-rich learning experiences through seven core areas: (1) developing an EdTech vision and mission statement, (2) identifying "tech-able" moments, (3) building your EdTech tool belt, (4) preparing for shifts in instructional models, (5) addressing concerns about equity and access, (6) recognizing the importance of media literacy and digital citizenship, and (7) planning with an artificial intelligence mindset.

Why Is This Essential?

Teachers of all grade levels and subjects can agree—having a plan is essential in every learning environment. Although planning may look different across content areas, the core idea is the same. As Gini Cunningham (2009) shares in *The New Teacher's Companion,* "Comprehensive plans increase the likelihood that lessons run smoothly, so that students receive quality instruction. By planning ahead, you are always set for the day" (p. 105). We know it is essential to have a plan for daily lessons, units of study, and individual interventions. Having a plan for technology integration and understanding how to shift plans if instructional delivery models change is equally critical for success in a tech-rich classroom.

I have used the phrase *tasks before apps* for the past decade in my conversations with educators. It has become such a core part of my vocabulary, I even used it for the title of my first book with ASCD. Placing tasks before apps means making learning front and center in your classroom. A video or a new digital tool might grab the attention of your students, but it is important to ensure it addresses a specific learning goal or enhances a learning experience you have designed for students.

Developing an EdTech Vision and Mission Statement

Most schools have a vision for the future and a mission statement that accompanies this goal. In *How to Help Your School Thrive Without Breaking the Bank,* John Gabriel and Paul Farmer (2009) state:

> Developing strong vision and mission statements can help stakeholders in your school reach . . . a common understanding. A vision is your school's goal—where you hope to see it in the future. The mission provides an overview of the steps planned to achieve that future. A vision is concise and easy to recall, whereas a mission is lengthier and more explanatory in nature. (p. 45)

Thoughtful technology integration may be part of your school or district's mission already, or you might find yourself working with a team this year to hone your vision and mission for the use of technology to support teaching and learning. Instead of giving you a Mad Libs–style template with fill-in-the-blank nouns and adjectives, I offer several questions to reflect on as you think about a vision (goal) and mission (steps to take) around EdTech:

- Why do you think technology has a place in the classroom?
- What will technology never replace?
- What value does educational technology provide?
- How does technology impact our students today? How will it impact students in the future?

- How will digital literacy and digital citizenship skills prepare our students for online interactions today, as well as for college and careers?

You might bring these questions and a "mission statement activity" to a group of educators in your school, such as a grade-level or department team. The questions might also provide a focus for conversations with mentors and mentees, families, students, and community members on the goals of using technology in your organization. The outcome of this exercise might not include a written paragraph but an opportunity to promote deeper thinking about the purpose behind using digital tools in your classroom, school, or district. It can help guide your purchasing decisions, professional development goals, and common commitment to using technology purposefully across your school community.

ISTE Education Leader Standard Indicator 3.2.a, Create a Shared Vision, states, "Engage education stakeholders in developing and adopting a shared vision for using technology to improve student success, informed by the learning sciences." ISTE Educator Standard Indicator 2.2.a, Advance a Shared Vision, calls educators to put ideas into action. It states, "Shape, advance and accelerate a shared vision for empowered learning with technology by engaging with education stakeholders."

Identifying "Tech-able" Moments

As a professional development facilitator, I often work with teams and individual teachers to review their goals for future instruction. We might unpack an upcoming unit together to determine its core goals, or we might look at an individual lesson and its components. Many teachers are familiar with the phrase *teachable moment,* which has appeared several times in earlier chapters of this book. A teachable moment describes an unplanned moment in a lesson or an activity when there is an opportunity to pause or take a quick detour. In these moments, you address an unexpected need instead of ignoring it or saving it to revisit at a later date.

A "tech-able moment" is a spin on this idea—a way of looking at a lesson, an activity, or a unit of study to identify moments when technology would enhance the learning experiences for students. The common theme for these tech-able moments is how they require us to examine the ways technology can address specific goals and obstacles, including how to differentiate for students, provide more ways for them to access content, boost participation and engagement, facilitate formative assessment, and extend learning experiences.

This enhancement could come in a few different areas, and the following questions can help guide you in your decision making:

- Can I use a digital resource (e.g., an explainer video, a podcast interview with an expert, a virtual reality experience) to build background knowledge?
- Will specific features of digital tools (e.g., voice-to-text, audio recordings, video responses) make it easier for students to share their learning?
- Can I use a tech-friendly strategy (e.g., polling, annotations, quick response to questions) to check for understanding more efficiently?
- Is there an option (e.g., virtual field trip, online sharing with a partner class) to extend this lesson in a way that was not possible in the past?

Building Your EdTech Tool Belt

Throughout this book, I have mentioned dozens of EdTech tools, and a comprehensive list appears in Appendix D. My intent is not to overwhelm you or make a case that every classroom and every teacher needs to use all of these—or even half of these—to be successful. In reality, it is just the opposite. You want to have a core set of tools you can use over and over again in a variety of contexts. Although you might introduce a new resource or tool to your students periodically, having a core set of tools in your belt is essential. The normal operating procedure in a classroom should include a set of tools students and teachers turn to regularly.

At the top of the list is a learning management system, or hub, students use to access content a teacher has shared with them. Students typically use this space to send content they have created back to their teacher. Often chosen by a school or district, these platforms could include Google Classroom and even Seesaw, which might not be considered true LMSs but are popular in K–12 classrooms for performing a similar function. The platform chosen as the hub for the distribution and organization of content sets a foundation and can further influence which tools you choose to add to your EdTech tool belt. Regarding the

LMS, I encourage you to "embrace your place," since this is a part of your EdTech tool belt often mandated to use and familiar to students from past school years or other courses. You will want to make sure any additional tools you introduce work well with this platform.

Your EdTech tool belt includes the go-to digital tools you use for teaching and learning. The following are a few general questions to help ensure the tools in your tool belt address your needs throughout the school year. These questions can help you review what you have already identified as a necessity and determine if something is missing. The needs of your students and the specific content you teach might lead you to add to the questions on this list:

- Is there a tool to help check for understanding so all students can share their learning?
- Have I identified open-ended creation tools that give students a space to create a product that demonstrates their learning?
- Will students be able to collaborate with their peers and work toward a common goal?
- Do these tools help students build transferable skills they can apply in a variety of contexts?
- Will these apps or websites work in the environment my students currently inhabit (home, school, hybrid)? Do they take connectivity, accessibility, and hardware into account?

Picking Great Tools

In addition to surveying the appendixes in this book and exploring the search bar on my website (https://classtechtips.com/blog), you may want to check out the EdSurge Product Index (go to https://index.edsurge.com or scan the QR code) if you are on the hunt for a specific EdTech tool.

EdSurge
Product
Index

Collaborating as a Team

In Chapter 6, we examined collaboration in the classroom primarily through the student lens. Collaborating as a team is essential for educators as well. Whether it's a grade-level team, department, or affinity group, the value of working together—especially when examining the common goal of thoughtful technology integration—can anchor your work. There are ways to use digital tools to create collections of curated resources in both asynchronous and synchronous professional collaboration.

Whether working asynchronously or synchronously, you can create a shared space where team members can add links, files, videos, and any other resource to create a collection. As you plan together, you might have

Is AI Your New Collaborator?

As a classroom teacher, I was fortunate to have supportive, accessible colleagues who were interested in collaborative planning. This is not the case in every school or district setting, particularly if you are the only person teaching a specific topic or subject area. As we explored in Chapter 3, you can use AI as a collaborator to help you plan your instruction in these situations. For example, you might share an idea and ask for feedback using prompts like the following:

- I am thinking of [idea] for my group of [description of students]. What are some pros and cons of this idea?

- I'm planning to teach [topic] using [activity]. What should I consider before introducing this to my group of students?

a specific focus, like making a collection of videos to help students study for a unit exam or for a grade level–wide research project on a single topic. Tools like Wakelet and Bublup are designed for users to create collections of resources and include options for adding collaborators. Alternatively, if your organization uses Google Drive or Microsoft OneDrive, you might decide to make a shared folder where colleagues can drop in resources throughout the school year.

Preparing for Shifts in Instructional Models

We could not have anticipated the rapid, emergency-based shifts to distance learning resulting from the COVID-19 pandemic, with millions of students suddenly learning at home and teachers supporting their students remotely. These *unknowns* are now *knowns,* and although rapid pivots in instructional models may feel unlikely, we can still plan for periodic shifts to distance learning as part of an overall plan for technology integration.

There are strong best practices *inside* the classroom that complement the needs of teaching and learning *outside* the classroom. To say the immediate shift to distance learning in the spring of 2020 was traumatic is an understatement; however, the classrooms that were able to transition to at-home learning with the least amount of disruption had a few key components in place. In addition to a central hub or platform for the distribution and collection of student work, these classrooms had invested time in routines that were scalable and adaptable to different learning environments. In "Keep It Simple, Schools," part of an *Educational Leadership* special report titled *A New Reality: Getting Remote Learning Right,* Justin Reich (2020) recommends, "As much as possible, schools should try to publish materials and check in with students using their existing technology infrastructure" (p. 7). For this transfer in delivery models to work effectively, a technology infrastructure must be in place, along with specific routines for using technology for teaching and learning.

Routines in a classroom setting are nothing new. A 1st grade teacher might establish routines for packing up at the end of the school day, or a 10th grade chemistry teacher might have routines for lab safety; they are rooted in the same idea. When developing classroom routines related to technology integration, you can take potential shifts in instructional models into consideration. You may find some routines work in the exact same way whether students participate at home or in a school building, while other classroom routines are adaptable to home learning with a few tweaks or changes. As you review current classroom routines related to technology use and establish new ones throughout the school year, here are several questions to consider:

- Do we have a central hub, platform, or learning management system to organize and distribute content to students?
- Are students familiar with how to navigate the online spaces we use on their own, or do they need a teacher by their side?
- Do we have scalable routines we can embrace and tweak if needed?
- How can we incorporate self-paced learning into a traditional, synchronous classroom environment?
- How do we currently check for understanding, and how would this look different if students were working from home instead of face-to-face in a physical classroom?

Addressing Concerns About Equity and Access

Concerns about equity and access should be critical considerations in planning any new initiative, and EdTech initiatives are no exception. The term *digital divide* describes the gaps in access to technology many students face. Issuing a device or a wireless internet hotspot for families does not automatically translate into fluency in navigating digital spaces. Although the access gap may be narrowing in certain areas as a result of more school-issued devices being distributed to families, we cannot assume that handing a device to a child is the same as providing strategic support and high-quality learning experiences with educational technology.

In "Leading for Equity: 5 Steps from Awareness to Commitment," Laura Aguada-Hallberg and Louise Santiago (2019) state, "As equity-centered leaders, we must identify biases and assumptions to avoid the pitfalls of the systems we are trying to transform" (para. 4). The following questions can guide your conversations around student experiences:

- Will students need devices outside the classroom to effectively complete work?
- What does connectivity look like in our community, and are there systems in place to support families in need?
- Do all students have opportunities to learn how to navigate online spaces and practice using tools some of their peers may be more familiar with?
- Are the vocabulary, imagery, and examples in a program or application our school adopts inclusive for all students?
- Am I asking students and families what they need to be successful when learning at school and at home?
- Do families and students know where to go to receive tech support, ask questions, and learn how to use technology for academic experiences? Is this a safe and welcoming space for them?

Providing opportunities for students, families, and faculty members to share their thoughts around these issues is more than posing a series of questions or sending home a survey. You might use these questions to spark a conversation, guide a discussion, and invite further questions to the table as you dive into the unique needs of your school community. Although it may feel natural to check in with families at the start of the school year, this commitment goes beyond a singular event or one-time meeting and should include periodic check-ins and an open invitation for ongoing conversations.

Recognizing the Importance of Media Literacy and Digital Citizenship

In the first chapter of this book, we looked at the value of helping students navigate online spaces with media literacy and digital citizenship front and center. As you develop plans for technology integration, a commitment to the inclusion of media literacy and digital citizenship is critical and requires regular planning and reflection. In the age of AI, students should understand how to evaluate digital spaces, question the authenticity of media, and determine the role of artificial intelligence in the resources they consume.

Making a plan for media literacy and digital citizenship includes addressing questions such as these:

- What does media literacy look like in the grade level or subject area I teach?
- How can I model digital citizenship skills to students?
- What expectations do I have for my students as digital citizens?
- What digital citizenship challenges do I expect to encounter when students work online?
- What is my commitment to preparing students as digital citizens? What do I value?
- How do I lead a conversation on AI-generated content with students?
- Are there cross-curricular connections that will help demonstrate a larger school commitment to media literacy and digital citizenship?

Your conversations around an EdTech vision and mission for your school or district may include digital citizenship and media literacy goals. Educators can incorporate these concepts into tech-able moments in which you clarify a misconception, evaluate a source, or look for an answer to an unexpected question during your lesson. As you explore these topics and commit to incorporating these skills into your work, it is important to acknowledge that success will not happen without a thoughtful plan to include digital citizenship and media literacy skills in your lessons and activities. Appendix E includes a list of digital citizenship resources to support this planning.

Planning with an Artificial Intelligence Mindset

How can you plan with AI in mind? In earlier chapters of this book, we've looked at ways to develop activity ideas, create compelling communications, and streamline repetitive tasks with generative AI tools. Leveraging the power of AI for instructional planning is just one aspect of *planning with an artificial intelligence mindset.* There is also the important work of planning for the known, anticipated, and unknown impacts of generative AI. Schools, districts, and education organizations will need to follow and address changes in this evolving space. Although in this book, our emphasis is on classroom-facing strategies and ways for educators to use generative AI tools, you may have conversations around this topic with your community at large.

Integrating AI in Your School

Educators exploring the role of AI in their learning environments may want to listen to my conversation with Dr. Marquita S. Blades on my (2023e) *Easy EdTech Podcast*. We discuss strategies for connecting your school's values to your AI framework, putting pedagogy before EdTech tools, and reframing the conversation around how AI can save teachers time. To listen, scan the QR code.

Easy EdTech Podcast: 239

Making a plan for addressing the impact of generative AI in your educational environment might include conversation-starting questions such as these:

- What should we include in a policy for AI use in our district?
- Which organizations and institutions (e.g., the Office of Educational Technology) should we turn to for guidance on the impact of AI in education?
- What frameworks or standards (e.g., the ISTE Standards) can help us envision appropriate uses for generative AI by students, teachers, and school leaders?

Final Thoughts

This chapter includes numerous questions to help you build a plan for technology integration in a variety of instructional models. Flexibility and reflection are key in any educational planning, and this is true of technology integration as well. Use the questions in this chapter and the EdTech essentials in this book to frame your goals for using educational technology throughout the school year. There is no one-size-fits-all approach to this work, and your own plan for EdTech will evolve over a semester or a school year. A proactive and responsive plan is critical, and although you may need to pivot if instructional or delivery models change, rooting your goals in the EdTech essentials described in this book can establish a strong foundation to help your students succeed in all learning environments.

Appendix A:
Essentials Versus Extras

This list summarizes some of the big ideas from each chapter to help you prioritize how to address the EdTech essentials in your own learning environment. You will also find some "extras" to explore to help you dive into the essentials more deeply.

Navigate Online Spaces Effectively

Essentials:

- Examine online text features to determine where to find quality information.
- Support student searches with think alouds and modeling.
- Demonstrate how to organize information with examples.

Extras:

- Create a scavenger hunt for students to locate information online as a way to practice navigation skills.
- Have students make a list of resources on a topic to practice evaluation skills.
- Encourage students to share their own mind maps and graphic organizers with classmates.

Curate Resources to Support Every Student

Essentials:

- Keep learning goals in mind to center resources on quality over quantity.
- Make sure resources are representative of and authentic to students.
- Curate to differentiate by choosing resources based on student needs.

Extras:

- Collaborate with colleagues to create curated lists of resources.
- Share curated resource lists with a professional learning network in online spaces.
- Curate lists of resources families can use to support their children at home.

Generate Ideas and Resources with Artificial Intelligence

Essentials:

- Use chatbots to gather ideas for upcoming activities.
- Tailor lesson plans and activity ideas to the needs of students.
- Differentiate instruction with the help of generative AI.

Extras:

- Create images to supplement a lesson.
- Explore the different outputs of generative AI.
- Practice prompt engineering with a variety of considerations.

Evaluate Digital Content with an AI Mindset

Essentials:

- Review online content with an understanding of sources and attribution.
- Use AI concepts to spark conversations on digital citizenship.

- Navigate digital spaces with an understanding of potential AI content generation.

Extras:

- Connect to English language arts skills such as close reading.
- Understand the potential uses for AI-generated audio and video content.
- Try a "fact check" activity with students and colleagues.

Explore the World with Students

Essentials:

- Introduce students to worlds different from their own.
- Provide students with opportunities to wonder and ask questions.
- Embrace virtual opportunities to transport students to new places.

Extras:

- Build connections with partner classes in different parts of the world to facilitate discussion and introduce new spaces.
- Incorporate regular events into your schedule for guest speakers.
- Create family-friendly experiences to extend virtual exploration beyond the classroom into the community.

Collaborate Across Digital Spaces

Essentials:

- Include opportunities for both asynchronous and synchronous collaboration.
- Create peer feedback loops that are connected to content goals.
- Incorporate discussions and use tech-friendly features as a value-add.

Extras:

- Invite classes from other parts of your school, district, or wider community to participate in collaborative activities.
- Incorporate opportunities for cross-generational collaboration with feedback loops from a partner organization.

- Provide asynchronous options for students who might choose a self-paced mode of contributing to a larger project.

Create Multimodal Artifacts of Learning

Essentials:

- Use exemplars to demonstrate expectations and set a vision for students.
- Design tasks that incorporate the value-add of tech-friendly features.
- Differentiate student process and product as needed.

Extras:

- Give students an opportunity to pitch their ideas for the type of product they would like to create.
- Use portfolios for students to collect their work over the course of a school year.
- Include cross-curricular creations in collaboration with colleagues in other subject areas or disciplines.

Assess to Check for Understanding and Pivot Instruction

Essentials:

- Identify your success criteria and what information you really need to know to determine student understanding.
- Create routines for assessment that students can use throughout the school year.
- Use the multiple features of digital tools to collect data from every student (e.g., text, audio, illustrations).

Extras:

- Make assessment social by using a platform where students can post responses to and celebrate the work of their peers.
- Use videoconferencing features, including chat spaces and break-out rooms, to check for understanding.
- Design personalized interventions for students by creating videos or screencast tutorials.

Share Student Creations in Big and Small Ways

Essentials:

- Provide opportunities for students to use speaking and listening skills to discuss their work and accomplishments.
- Celebrate small and big moments in digital spaces.
- Incorporate visual communication into a plan for student sharing.

Extras:

- Carve out time for weekly or daily sharing of student accomplishments.
- Connect sharing to conversations about personal branding and social media.
- Give students an option to share in public, online spaces (with permission).

Connect Students to Authentic Audiences

Essentials:

- Tailor tasks to students' expressed interests.
- Begin with a clear vision of an audience when introducing extended learning experiences to students.
- State a clear purpose for student creations (e.g., persuade, entertain, inform).

Extras:

- Provide students with an opportunity to research and choose an audience for their work.
- Connect with a partner class to work with throughout the school year to share updates and accomplishments.
- Use social media–style video creations and posts as inspiration for student work products.

Transfer Skills Across Digital Spaces

Essentials:

- Incorporate opportunities for students to build independence in digital spaces.
- Question students to help them troubleshoot tech issues.
- Model problem solving and adaptability for students.

Extras:

- Introduce students to opportunities for independent learning with a mentor.
- Invite students to share problem-solving strategies or helpful tips with their peers at weekly meetings.
- Create tech support opportunities for students to increase independence.

Plan for Tech-Rich Learning Experiences

Essentials:

- Create an EdTech vision and mission statement.
- Introduce a platform or hub to centralize distribution and collection of learning resources.
- Review and revisit gaps in equity and access.

Extras:

- Hold digital tool belt events where colleagues share a new EdTech tool or resource and how it has made an impact in their classroom.
- Locate a partner school or organization with a similar EdTech vision and mission statement for collaborative planning.
- Design events for family and community learning to help build skills to support tech use in multiple learning environments.

Appendix B:
Resources for Taking Action

Goal Setting —————————————————————————— 152

Partner-in-Tech Planning Page ————————————————— 153

Building My Tool Belt ————————————————————— 154

Planning Page for Generating AI Prompts ——————————— 155

Self-Assessment #1 ————————————————————— 156

Self-Assessment #2 ————————————————————— 158

These forms are available for download at https://www.ascd.org/edtech
-essentials-resources (or scan QR code).

*EdTech
Essentials*
Resources

Goal Setting

What is your personal EdTech mission?

What are your strengths in EdTech integration?

Goal timeline:

- This week:

- This month:

- This year:

Partner-in-Tech Planning Page

Partner #1:

Partner #2:

What is our common struggle?

What would we like to accomplish?

Three steps to help us accomplish our goal:

    1.

    2.

    3.

Our timeline:

Start:

Finish:

Building My Tool Belt

What tools are currently in my tool belt?

What tools are on my radar but not in my tool belt?

What is missing from my tool belt (i.e., I need a tool that can . . .)?

What tools will I try out next? (Include my "why.")

Planning Page for Generating AI Prompts

What are you trying to create or figure out with the help of a chatbot?

What type of *format* would you like to generate (e.g., paragraph, list, poem)?

What is the *tone* you would like to convey (e.g., friendly, professional, supportive)?

What details can you provide about the *context* (e.g., audience, prior knowledge, example)?

Self-Assessment #1

What are your comfort and confidence levels with the EdTech essentials? (Use a scale of 1 to 10 to indicate low to high.)

Navigate online spaces effectively.

Comfort and confidence level: _____

Curate resources to support every student.

Comfort and confidence level: _____

Generate ideas and resources with artificial intelligence.

Comfort and confidence level: _____

Evaluate digital content with an AI mindset.

Comfort and confidence level: _____

Explore the world with students.

Comfort and confidence level: _____

Collaborate across digital spaces.

Comfort and confidence level: _____

Create multimodal artifacts of learning.

Comfort and confidence level: _____

Assess to check for understanding and pivot instruction.

Comfort and confidence level: _____

Share student creations in big and small ways.

Comfort and confidence level: _____

Connect students to authentic audiences.

Comfort and confidence level: _____

Transfer skills across digital spaces.

Comfort and confidence level: _____

Plan for tech-rich learning experiences.

Comfort and confidence level: _____

Self-Assessment #2

In what areas are you thriving, shining, growing?

- *Thriving:* excelling in one aspect of the essential, ready to support a colleague
- *Shining:* doing a great job, ready to share a success story
- *Growing:* working with purpose toward accomplishing a goal, searching for support or a partner-in-tech

Navigate online spaces effectively.

- Thriving:
- Shining:
- Growing:

Curate resources to support every student.

- Thriving:
- Shining:
- Growing:

Generate ideas and resources with artificial intelligence.

- Thriving:
- Shining:
- Growing:

Evaluate digital content with an AI mindset.

- Thriving:
- Shining:
- Growing:

Explore the world with students.

- Thriving:
- Shining:
- Growing:

Collaborate across digital spaces.

- Thriving:
- Shining:
- Growing:

Create multimodal artifacts of learning.

- Thriving:
- Shining:
- Growing:

Assess to check for understanding and pivot instruction.

- Thriving:
- Shining:
- Growing:

Share student creations in big and small ways.

- Thriving:
- Shining:
- Growing:

Connect students to authentic audiences.

- Thriving:
- Shining:
- Growing:

Transfer skills across digital spaces.

- Thriving:
- Shining:
- Growing:

Plan for tech-rich learning experiences.

- Thriving:
- Shining:
- Growing:

Appendix C:
Monica's Favorite Prompts
to Use with Chatbots

ChatGPT
Book

To download a PDF ebook with more favorite prompts, please visit classtechtips.com/chatgptbook or scan the QR code.

Communication

Use the following prompts to draft emails that you can tailor to the recipient. This is a great way to get a jump start on crafting emails or to set up an email template. When you paste your email draft, remove personal information like names.

- Proofread my email for grammar, spelling, and punctuation errors [paste email draft].
- Suggest ways to rephrase or restructure my sentences to improve clarity and coherence [paste email draft].
- Rewrite this email so it is more [adjective] [paste email draft].
- Write a thank-you email to a family member who [way they helped].
- Write an email to check in with [person] about [topic] to see if they want to schedule a meeting.

Activity Ideas

If you are teaching something new or want to introduce a new topic to a group of students, try out one of the following prompts. These can help you kick off a new unit or get students excited about a series of lessons.

- What are some fun ways to introduce [topic] to [grade level]?
- Write a model essay on [topic] that includes [features].
- Write a song in the style of [artist/genre] that teaches students about [topic].
- Provide some examples of open-ended questions to include in a student survey about [topic].
- Explain [topic] with a metaphor so it is easy for [grade level] to understand.

Vocabulary Support

There are lots of ways to introduce new vocabulary to students, and the following chatbot prompts for teachers can help your vocabulary instruction. These are particularly useful if you are working with a group of students with various levels of background knowledge on a topic.

- Explain the meaning of [word] and put it in a sentence.
- Write a song that reinforces the meaning of [word].
- Write a list of synonyms and antonyms for [word].
- Make a list of important vocabulary words related to [topic].
- Give me a vocabulary word related to [topic] for each letter of the alphabet.

Resource Gathering

To gather helpful resources for your students, you can use prompts that suggest lessons, prompts, and other recommendations for students. These prompts can come in handy for teachers looking for resources to share with their entire class or just a selection of students.

- Recommend [genre] books about [topic] for [grade level].
- Write [number] kid-friendly jokes about [topic].
- Suggest some tools or resources to help me create interactive presentations for my students.

- My students are interested in [topic]. Make a list of resources that connect to their [interest].

Productivity

Although all these prompts can help you save time, these fall more into the productivity category. They can help streamline time-consuming tasks or address other issues related to productivity. Share your favorite productivity prompt with a colleague.

- Create an agenda for a meeting with [group] about [topic].
- Summarize my notes from a meeting on [topic] [paste your notes].
- Make me a spreadsheet for tracking my daily habits with columns for [date], [habit #1], [habit #2], and [habit #3].
- Use boldface, italics, and underlining to highlight key information and draw attention to important points [paste your writing].
- Turn this list into a table with one column for [category] and another column for [category].

Appendix D:
100+ EdTech Tools and Resources for Teachers and Students

The following list includes tools mentioned throughout the chapters of this book, along with a few extras. Many are free, while others have a freemium, trial, or paid model. Some of these tools were featured in multiple chapters, and many address more than one of the essentials explored in this book. In addition to the tools listed here, throughout the book and in Appendix E you will find recommendations for books, learning opportunities, podcast episodes, organizations, and online resources to support your work this year.

Note: I often partner and work behind the scenes with popular and growing EdTech companies, including a few featured here. You will want to make sure any EdTech tools you use are approved by your school or district and meet requirements for the Children's Online Privacy Protection Act (COPPA), the General Data Protection Regulation (GDPR), or state and local requirements for use with students.

Tools to Help Students Explore the World
- 360schools (virtual reality)
- AirPano (virtual reality)
- CoSpaces Edu (augmented reality)

- Google Arts & Culture (global content)
- Google Maps (interactive maps)
- Google Maps Treks (interactive guides)
- Merge Cube (augmented reality)
- YouVisit (interactive guides)

Tools for Student Creators

- Adobe Express (graphic design, website building, movie making)
- Adobe Podcast (podcasting)
- Adobe Premiere Rush (video creation)
- Book Creator (ebook creation)
- Canva (graphic design)
- Clips (mobile-friendly movies)
- Drawp for School (creative projects)
- Explain Everything (explainer videos)
- GarageBand (podcasting)
- Google Docs (word processor)
- Google Drawings (mind mapping)
- Google Slides (presentation tool)
- iMovie (movie making)
- Keynote (presentation tool)
- Microsoft Word (word processor)
- Pages (word processor)
- PicCollage (graphic design)
- Soundtrap for Education (podcasting)
- Tinkercad (3D modeling)
- WeVideo (movie making)

Tools to Build Portfolios and Share Collections of Resources

- bulb (portfolio)
- Bublup (collections)
- Google Sites (website building)
- LiveBinders (notebook)
- Microsoft Sway (landing page)
- QR Stuff (QR code generator)
- Smore (website building)
- SpacesEDU (portfolio)
- Wakelet (collections)

Tools to Boost Productivity

- Asana (project management)
- Brain.fm (time management/focus)
- Evernote (note taking)
- FigJam (collaborative whiteboard)
- Forest (time management/focus)
- Google Keep (note taking)
- Google Sheets (spreadsheet)
- Grammarly (editing)
- Idea Sketch (mind mapping)
- Loom (screencasting)
- Microsoft Lists (task management)
- Microsoft OneNote (notebook)
- Monday (project management)
- Mural (brainstorming)
- Screencastify (screencasting)
- Trello (project management)

Generative AI Chatbots

- Gemini (rebranded from Bard)
- ChatGPT
- Claude
- Perplexity.ai

Assessment Tools for Teachers

- Conker (AI quiz question generator)
- Flip (video responses)
- Google Forms (survey tool)
- Kahoot! (questioning)
- Kaizena (feedback)
- Microsoft Forms (survey tool)
- Mote (audio commenting)
- Padlet (collaborative posting)
- Popplet (mind mapping)
- Pressto AI Writing Assistant (writing prompt generator)
- Socrative (quizzing)
- Vocaroo (audio recording)
- Whiteboard.chat (whiteboard)
- Writable (AI feedback)

Presentation Tools for Teachers

- Curipod (AI-supported presentation generator)
- Lumio (interactive presentation)
- Mentimeter (polling)
- Microsoft Whiteboard (brainstorming)
- Nearpod (interactive presentation)
- Pear Deck (interactive presentation)
- Poll Everywhere (polling)
- Scribblar (whiteboard)
- simpleshow (explainer video maker)

Supplemental Curriculum Resources

- BrainPOP (explainer videos)
- *Brains On!* (podcast)
- Diffit (AI-powered resource creator)
- Empatico (SEL resource)
- Flocabulary (video library)
- Khan Academy (video tutorials)
- MagicSchool (AI-powered resource creator)
- Newsela (current events articles)
- PebbleGo (informational articles)
- Quiver (augmented reality)
- Spotify (podcast platform)
- Storyline Online (read-aloud videos)
- Ted-Ed (platform with educational videos)
- Vimeo (video platform)
- Wikipedia (crowdsourced encyclopedia)
- *Wow in the World* (podcast)
- YouTube (video platform)
- zSpace (augmented/virtual reality)

Learning and Content Management Tools

- Canvas (learning management system)
- Dropbox (cloud-based sharing)
- Google Classroom (content management system)
- Google Drive (cloud-based sharing)
- Seesaw (portfolio and journaling tool)

Communication and Social Tools

- Google Meet (videoconferencing)
- Instagram (social media)
- Microsoft Teams (collaboration and videoconferencing)
- Moodle (learning management system)
- Otus (learning management system)
- PowerSchool Schoology Learning (learning management system)
- Slack (communication)

Appendix E:
Additional Resources

Navigate Online Spaces
- Creating Community in Online Classrooms (ISTE U Course): https://iste.org/courses/creating-community-in-online-classrooms
- Ensuring Equity and Inclusion in Online Learning (ISTE U Course): https://iste.org/courses/ensuring-equity-inclusion-online-learning

Artificial Intelligence
- *AI in the Classroom* (Jump Start Guide) by Nancye Blair Black (ISTE, 2023)
- Artificial Intelligence Explorations for Educators (ISTE U course): https://iste.org/courses/artificial-intelligence-explorations-for -educators
- *Using AI Chatbots to Enhance Planning and Instruction* (Quick Reference Guide) by Monica Burns (ASCD, 2023)
- ISTE information and resources on AI: https://iste.org/ai

Explore, Create, Connect, and Share
- *40 Ways to Inject Creativity into Your Classroom with Adobe Spark* by Ben Forta and Monica Burns (Elevate Books Edu, 2019)

- *Awesome Sauce: Create Videos to Inspire Students, Engage Parents and Save You Time* by Josh Stock (ISTE, 2020)
- *Engaging Students in Reading All Types of Text* (Quick Reference Guide) by Pam Allyn and Monica Burns (ASCD, 2021)
- *Flip Your Classroom, Revised Edition: Reach Every Student in Every Class Every Day* by Jonathan Bergmann and Aaron Sams (ASCD/ ISTE, 2023)
- *Learning First, Technology Second in Practice: New Strategies, Research and Tools for Student Success* by Liz Kolb (ISTE, 2020)
- *Learning Transported: Augmented, Virtual and Mixed Reality for All Classrooms* by Jaime Donally (ISTE, 2018)
- *The Perfect Blend: A Practical Guide to Designing Student-Centered Learning Experiences* by Michele Eaton (ISTE, 2020)
- *Storytelling with Purpose: Digital Projects to Ignite Student Curiosity* by Michael Hernandez (ISTE, 2024)
- *Teach Boldly: Using Edtech for Social Good* by Jennifer Williams (ISTE, 2019)

Digital Literacy and Computational Thinking

- Digital Literacy in the Classroom (ISTE U course): https://iste.org /courses/digital-literacy-in-the-classroom
- *Digital Literacy Made Simple: Strategies for Building Skills Across the Curriculum* by Jenna Kammer and Lauren Hays (ISTE, 2023)
- *No Fear Coding, Second Edition: Computational Thinking Across the K–5 Curriculum* by Heidi Williams (ISTE, 2021)
- ISTE information and resources on computational thinking: https:// iste.org/computational-thinking

Technology Integration

- *Classroom Technology Tips* (Quick Reference Guide) by Monica Burns (ASCD, 2020)
- *Distance Learning Essentials* (Quick Reference Guide) by Monica Burns (ASCD, 2020)
- *Integrating Technology in the Classroom, Second Edition: Tools to Meet the Needs of Every Student* by Boni Hamilton (ISTE, 2018)
- *Tasks Before Apps: Designing Rigorous Learning in a Tech-Rich Classroom* by Monica Burns (ASCD, 2017)

- *Tech for Teacher Wellness: Strategies for a Healthy Life and Sustainable Career* by Meredith Masar Boullion (ISTE, 2023)

Digital Citizenship

- Digital Citizenship in Action (ISTE U course): https://iste.org /courses/digital-citizenship
- *Digital Citizenship in Action, Second Edition: Empowering Students to Engage in Online Communities* by Kristen Mattson (ISTE, 2024)
- *Fact vs. Fiction: Teaching Critical Thinking Skills in the Age of Fake News* by Jennifer LaGarde and Darren Hudgins (ISTE, 2018)
- *Teaching Students to Decode the World: Media Literacy and Critical Thinking Across the Curriculum* by Chris Sperry and Cyndy Scheibe (ASCD, 2022)
- Be Internet Awesome: https://beinternetawesome.withgoogle.com /en_us/
- DigCitCommit: digcitcommit.org
- Digital Citizenship Curriculum from Common Sense Media: https:// www.commonsense.org/education/digital-citizenship/curriculum
- ISTE information and resources on digital citizenship: https://iste .org/digital-citizenship
- Project Look Sharp: https://projectlooksharp.org

References

Aguada-Hallberg, L., & Santiago, L. (2019). Leading for equity: 5 steps from awareness to commitment. *ASCD Express, 14*(23). http://www.ascd.org/ascd-express/vol14 /num23/leading-for-equity-5-steps-from-awareness-to-commitment.aspx

Allyn, P., & Burns, M. (2021). *Engaging students in reading all types of text* (Quick reference guide). ASCD.

Anderson, L. W., & Krathwohl, D. R. (Eds.). (2001). *A taxonomy for learning, teaching, and assessing: A revision of Bloom's taxonomy of educational objectives.* Longman.

Anderson, M. (2016). *Learning to choose, choosing to learn: The key to student motivation and achievement.* ASCD.

ASCD. (n.d.). The whole child. Retrieved from http://www.ascd.org/programs/The-Whole -Child/Engaged.aspx

Bieser, J. (2023, February 20). How can AI support human creativity? Here's what a new study found. World Economic Forum. https://www.weforum.org/agenda/2023/02 /ai-can-catalyze-and-inhibit-your-creativity-here-is-how/

Burns, M. (2017). *#FormativeTech: Meaningful, sustainable, and scalable formative assessment with technology.* Corwin.

Burns, M. (2018). *Tasks before apps: Designing rigorous learning in a tech-rich classroom.* ASCD.

Burns, M. (Host). (2020a, June 16). How to incorporate computational thinking in any subject with Jorge Valenzuela (No. 66) [Audio podcast episode]. In *Easy EdTech Podcast.* https://classtechtips.com/2020/06/16/computational-thinking-066

Burns, M. (Host). (2020b, October 6). Teaching tech fluency with icons in early childhood classrooms with Pana Asavavatana (No. 82) [Audio podcast episode]. In *Easy EdTech Podcast.* https://classtechtips.com/2020/10/06/icons-in-early-childhood-082

Burns, M. (Host). (2021, September 7). Useful tips for finding podcasts to enhance content with Jeff Glade (No. 128) [Audio podcast episode]. In *Easy EdTech Podcast.* https:// classtechtips.com/2021/09/07/finding-podcasts-128/

Burns, M. (Host). (2022a, May 31). Creating real audiences for student projects with Jennifer Hall (No. 165) [Audio podcast episode]. In *Easy EdTech Podcast.* https:// classtechtips.com/2022/05/31/student-projects-165

Burns, M. (Host). (2022b, November 22). Help students take ownership of their learning with Kendra Grant (No. 190) [Audio podcast episode]. In *Easy EdTech Podcast.* https://classtechtips.com/2022/11/22/students-take-ownership-190

Burns, M. (2022c). Using "I wonder . . ." books to capture questions. Book Creator blog. https://bookcreator.com/2022/03/using-i-wonder-books-to-capture-questions/

Burns, M. (Host). (2022d, June 21). What teens actually need to be tech-savvy with Dr. Cassidy Puckett (No. 168) [Audio podcast episode]. In *Easy EdTech Podcast*. https://classtechtips.com/2022/06/21/tech-savvy-teens-168/

Burns, M. (Host). (2023a, November 14). 4 types of AI tools every teacher should know about (No. 241) [Audio podcast episode]. In *Easy EdTech Podcast*. https://classtechtips.com/2023/11/14/types-of-ai-tools-241

Burns, M. (Host). (2023b, July 18). The power of icon literacy with Debbie Tannenbaum (No. 224) [Audio podcast episode]. In *Easy EdTech Podcast*. https://classtechtips.com/2023/07/18/icon-literacy-224

Burns, M. (Host). (2023c, June 13). Power of pausing: Reflection activities for your classroom with Rachelle Dené Poth (No. 219) [Audio podcast episode]. In *Easy EdTech Podcast*. https://classtechtips.com/2023/06/13/reflection-activities-219

Burns, M. (Host). (2023d, June 27). Strengthen SEL skills during any project with Michele Haiken (No. 221) [Audio podcast episode]. In *Easy EdTech Podcast*. https://classtechtips.com/2023/06/27/sel-skills-221

Burns, M. (Host). (2023e, October 31). Tips for making an AI framework for your school with Dr. Marquita S. Blades (No. 239) [Audio podcast episode]. In *Easy EdTech Podcast*. https://classtechtips.com/2023/10/31/ai-framework-239

Burns, M. (Host). (2023f, May 9). Uncheatable assessments and the role of digital storytelling in the classroom with Michael Hernandez (No. 214) [Audio podcast episode]. In *Easy EdTech Podcast*. https://classtechtips.com/2023/05/09/uncheatable-assessments-214

Burns, M. (2023g). *Using AI chatbots to enhance planning and instruction* (Quick reference guide). ASCD & ISTE.

Burns, M. (Host). (2023h, October 3). Using tech to help students tell their stories with Pam Allyn (No. 235) [Audio podcast episode]. In *Easy EdTech Podcast*. https://classtechtips.com/2023/10/03/help-students-tell-their-stories-235

Burns, M. (Host). (2024, January 2). Leveraging ChatGPT for customized learning with Sarah Wysocki (No. 248) [Audio podcast episode]. In *Easy EdTech Podcast*. https://classtechtips.com/2024/01/02/customized-learning-248

Butler, M. (n.d.). The 9 habits of highly successful content creators. *Hubspot*. https://blog.hubspot.com/marketing/5-habits-of-highly-successful-content-creators-list

CareerExplorer. (n.d.). What does an app developer do? https://www.careerexplorer.com/careers/app-developer

Children's Online Privacy Protection Act of 1998. 15 U.S.C. §§ 6501–6506.

Collaborative for Social and Emotional Learning (CASEL). (n.d.). *Fundamentals of SEL*. https://casel.org/fundamentals-of-sel

Cunningham, G. (2009). *The new teacher's companion: Practical wisdom for succeeding in the classroom*. ASCD.

Dell'Acqua, F., McFowland, E., Mollick, E. R., Lifshitz-Assaf, H., Kellogg, K., Rajendran, S., Krayer, L., Candelon, F., & Lakhani, K. R. (2023, September 15). Navigating the jagged technological frontier: Field experimental evidence of the effects of AI on knowledge worker productivity and quality. Harvard Business School Technology & Operations Mgt. Unit Working Paper No. 24-013. https://ssrn.com/abstract=4573321

Eapen, T. T., Finkenstadt, D. J., Folk, J., & Venkataswamy, L. (2023). How generative AI can augment human creativity. *Harvard Business Review*. https://hbr.org/2023/07/how-generative-ai-can-augment-human-creativity

Entrepreneur. (n.d.). Branding [definition]. Entrepreneur Media. Retrieved December 11, 2023, from https://www.entrepreneur.com/encyclopedia/branding

Fisher, D. B., & Frey, N. (2011). *The purposeful classroom: How to structure lessons with learning goals in mind*. ASCD.

Fisher, D. B., & Frey, N. (2014). *Checking for understanding: Formative assessment techniques for your classroom*. ASCD.

Gabriel, J. G., & Farmer, P. C. (2009). *How to help your school thrive without breaking the bank*. ASCD.

Grant, K., & Perez, L. (2022). *Dive into UDL: Immersive practices to develop expert learners* (2nd ed.). ISTE.

Greenstein, L. (2010). *What teachers really need to know about formative assessment*. ASCD.

Haiken, M. (2020). *Podcasting for students* (Jump start guide). ISTE.

Hardie, E. (2019.) *The relevant classroom: 6 steps to foster real-world learning*. ASCD.

Hernandez, M. (2024). *Storytelling with purpose: Digital projects to ignite student curiosity*. ISTE.

ISTE. (2016). ISTE standards for students. https://www.iste.org/standards/students

ISTE. (2017). ISTE standards for educators. https://iste.org/standards/educators

ISTE. (2018). ISTE standards for education leaders. https://iste.org/standards/education-leaders

ISTE. (2020). ISTE standards for coaches. www.iste.org/standards/coaches

Kaufman, S. B. (2017, July 24). Schools are missing what matters about learning. *The Atlantic*. https://www.theatlantic.com/education/archive/2017/07/the-underrated-gift-of-curiosity/534573/

Merriam-Webster. (n.d.). Collaborate. In *Merriam-Webster.com dictionary*. Retrieved December 11, 2023, from https://www.merriam-webster.com/dictionary/collaborate

Merriam-Webster. (n.d.). Essential. In *Merriam-Webster.com dictionary*. Retrieved December 11, 2023, from https://www.merriam-webster.com/dictionary/essential

Mohsin, M. (2020). 10 TikTok statistics that you need to know in 2021. https://www.oberlo.com/blog/tiktok-statistics

Mollick, E. R., & Mollick, L. (2023, September 23). Assigning AI: Seven approaches for students, with prompts. Wharton School of the University of Pennsylvania & Wharton Interactive. http://dx.doi.org/10.2139/ssrn.4475995

NAMLE. (n.d.). *About NAMLE*. National Association for Media Literacy Education. https://namle.net/about

Ness, M. (2018a). Improving reading comprehension with think-alouds. *We Are Teachers*. https://www.weareteachers.com/think-alouds-reading-comprehension

Ness, M. (2018b). *Think big with think alouds, grades K–5: A three-step planning process that develops strategic readers*. Corwin.

Poth, R. D. (2023). Building a learning community from day one. *Edutopia*. https://www.edutopia.org/article/student-learning-communities-day-one/

Puckett, C. (2022). *Redefining geek: Bias and the five hidden habits of tech-savvy teens*. University of Chicago Press.

Reich, J. (2020, Summer). Keep it simple, schools. *An Educational Leadership Special Report: A New Reality: Getting Remote Learning Right, 77*, 2–5. http://www.ascd.org/publications/educational-leadership/summer20/vol77/num10/Keep-It-Simple,-Schools.aspx

Roake, J., & Varlas, L. (2013, December). More than words: Developing core speaking and listening skills. *ASCD Education Update, 55*(12), 1, 4–5.

Robinson, K. (2006, June). *Do schools kill creativity?* TED. https://www.ted.com/talks/sir_ken_robinson_do_schools_kill_creativity/transcript

Satariano, A., & Mozur, P. (2023, February 7). The people onscreen are fake. The disinformation is real. *New York Times*. https://www.nytimes.com/2023/02/07/technology/artificial-intelligence-training-deepfake.html

Spotify. (n.d.). 2019 wrapped for podcasters: Your year on Spotify. https://podcasters.spotify.com/blog/podcaster-wrapped-2019

Stone, E. (2017). The science behind the growing importance of collaboration. *KelloggInsight*. https://insight.kellogg.northwestern.edu/article/the-science-behind-the-growing-importance-of-collaboration

Stoppard, L. (2020, March 3). Everyone's a curator now. *New York Times*. https://www.nytimes.com/2020/03/03/style/curate-buzzword.html

Sullo, B. (2009). *The motivated student: Unlocking the enthusiasm for learning.* ASCD.

Tomlinson, C. A. (2017). *How to differentiate instruction in academically diverse classrooms* (3rd ed.). ASCD.

Tomlinson, C. A., & Moon, T. R. (2013). *Assessment and student success in a differentiated classroom.* ASCD.

Tyson, K., Hintz, A., & Hernandez, K. (2014, November). How to foster deep listening. *Educational Leadership, 72*(3). http://www.ascd.org/publications/educational-leadership/nov14/vol72/num03/How-to-Foster-Deep-Listening.aspx

U.S. Department of Education, Office of Educational Technology. (2023, May). *Artificial intelligence and the future of teaching and learning: Insights and recommendations.* https://tech.ed.gov/files/2023/05/ai-future-of-teaching-and-learning-report.pdf

Valenzuela, J. (2020). *Rev up robotics: Real-world computational thinking in the K–8 classroom.* ISTE.

Vinchon, F., Lubart, T., Bartolotta, S., Gironnay, V., Botella, M., Bourgeois-Bougrine, S., Burkhardt, J.-M., Bonnardel, N., Corazza, G. E., Glăveanu, V., Hanchett Hanson, M., Ivcevic, Z., Karwowski, M., Kaufman, J. C., Okada, T., Reiter-Palmon, R., & Gaggioli, A. (2023). Artificial intelligence & creativity: A manifesto for collaboration. *Journal of Creative Behavior.* https://doi.org/10.1002/jocb.597

Walton Family Foundation. (2023, March 1). ChatGPT used by teachers more than students, new survey from Walton Family Foundation finds. https://www.waltonfamilyfoundation.org/chatgpt-used-by-teachers-more-than-students-new-survey-from-walton-family-foundation-finds

Williams, J. (2019). *Teach boldly: Using EdTech for social good.* ISTE.

Wilson, D., & Conyers, M. (2016). *Teaching students to drive their brains: Metacognitive strategies, activities, and lesson ideas.* ASCD.

Wysocki, S. (2023, November 1). 3 ways to keep middle school students engaged. *Edutopia.* https://www.edutopia.org/article/engaging-middle-schoolers-learning

YouTube. (n.d.). YouTube for press. blog.youtube/press

Index

Note: Page references followed by an italic *f* indicates information contained in figures.

access, equitable, 141–142
access and empathy, 56–57
accessibility, 11
accuracy, 49
action items, 74
adaptability, 132
Adobe Express, 20, 89, 90, 91, 111, 113
Adobe Firefly, 84
Adobe Podcast, 88
app developer thinking, 130–131
Apple Accessibility Overview, 11
applications, curating, 26
artifacts of learning, student. *See* creating
  multimodal artifacts of learning
artificial intelligence (AI), 146. *See also*
  chatbots, generative AI; generative AI
  chatbot queries, 12, 15–16, 17*f*
  as collaborator for instructional
    design, 140
  creativity in age of AI, 83–85
  essential ideas and extra tips, 146
  to give feedback to students, 103
  planning instruction and, 143–144
  for resource curation, 30–31, 33
  updated AI resources, 46
  using to pivot instruction after
    assessment, 105–106

assessment
  about, 97–98
  benefits of technology use in, 103–104
  chatbots for activity design, 39
  essential ideas and extra tips, 148
  formative assessment, 98–103
  generating assessment questions
    with AI, 100
  tech-friendly interventions, 104–106
*Assessment and Student Success in a
  Differentiated Classroom* (Tomlinson
  & Moon), 103
assessment tools for teachers, 165
asset mindset, 133
asynchronous assessment, 104
asynchronous collaboration, 70–71
asynchronous connection, 63–64
asynchronous discussions, 76
audience, connecting student work to
  about, 116–118
  author's purpose, 120–122
  beginning with audience in mind,
    118–119
  essential ideas and extra tips, 149
  for everyday learning, 122–123
  relevance, 123–124
  social justice, 119–120

audio-based discussions, 77
audio content, 10
audio content curating, 26, 27*f*
audio creations, 86–88
audio feedback, 75–76
augmented reality (AR), 59–61
authenticity, 50–51
authority, 48–49
author's purpose, 118, 120–122
autonomy, 126–128

background knowledge, 29
basic computing skills, 21–22
Book Creator, 19, 20, 59, 91, 93, 103, 112
books, digital, 93
Brain.fm, 14
BrainPOP, 105
brainstorming, 51
branding, student, 114–115

Calm, 14
Canva for Education, 90
Canvas, 111
chatbots, generative AI. *See also*
  artificial intelligence (AI)
    activity ideas prompts, 161
    to brainstorm potential audiences,
      119
    collaboration with, 78–80
    common chatbot terms, 37
    communication prompts, 160
    to curate content, 30–31, 33
    for differentiating instruction, 105
    for exploring the world, 56
    generating assessment questions
      with, 100
    to give feedback to students, 103
    for idea and resource generation,
      38–40
    for image generation, 40–42
    for information organization, 43
    linking computational thinking to
      subject instruction, 134
    list of, 165
    originality reports, 52
    presentation creator tools, 44
    productivity prompts, 162
    prompt engineering, 37, 84

chatbots, generative AI—(*continued*)
    prompts, 37, 41–42, 44–45, 84–85,
      160–162
    queries, 12, 15–16, 17*f*
    question generator tools, 44
    resource gathering prompts, 161–162
    time-saving uses for, 42–43
    tools for assessment, 101
    and virtual field trips, 64
    vocabulary support prompts, 161
ChatGPT, 12, 15, 40
checking for understanding. *See*
  assessment
*Checking for Understanding: Formative
  Assessment Techniques for Your
  Classroom* (Fisher & Frey), 98–99
checklists, 95
Children's Online Privacy Protection
  Act (COPPA), 12
Chromebook Accessibility, 11
classroom routines and procedures,
  140–141
Claude, 15
Clips, 91, 110, 111
collaboration
    about, 67–69
    asynchronous, 70–71
    with chatbots, 78–80
    EdTech tools and resources,
      139–140
    essential ideas and extra tips,
      147–148
    models for, 69–71
    peer feedback, 71–76
    remote, 69–70
    role-based, 69–70
    shared-screen, 69–70
    spaces for, 71
    synchronous, 70–71
Collaborative for Academic, Social, and
  Emotional Learning (CASEL), 58–59
comic strips, 89–90
communication and social tools, 167
communication prompts, 160
community, 117. *See also* audience,
  connecting student work to
computational thinking, 132–134
Conker, 44, 101

connecting student work to audience. *See* audience, connecting student work to
connections and empathy, 57–58
consumers, 9
content categories, 25–27, 27*f*, 28*f*
content creators, 117
content differentiation, 93
content management (curation)
    about, 23–24
    chatbots for, 30–31, 43
    content categories, 25–27, 27*f*–28*f*
    content organization and distribution, 31–35, 43
    content selection, 28–29
    differentiation and, 24
    students as curators, 34–35
    tools for, 31–32
content management systems, 31–32
content management tools, 166
COVID-19 pandemic, 140
creating multimodal artifacts of learning
    about, 81–83
    analog/offline creations, 92
    audio creations, 86–88
    checklists and rubrics, 95
    comic strips, 89–90
    creativity in age of AI, 83–85
    differentiation of process and product, 92–94
    essential ideas and extra tips, 148
    exemplars, 94–95
    graphic organizers, 95–96
    infographics, 89
    multimedia creations, 90–91
    open-ended creation tools, 91–92
    podcasts, 87
    process emphasis in, 51–52, 85
    sharing as culminating activity, 112–113
    support for success, 94–96
    text creations, 88–89
    types of tech-enhanced student creations, 85–91
    visual creations, 89–90
creation tools, open-ended, 91–92
creativity, 82, 83–85

culminating activity, sharing as, 112–113
curation. *See* content management (curation); resource curation
curiosity, 54–55
Curipod, 44, 101
curriculum resources and tools, 166

deep-dive searches, 12–13
design logic, 20
developer thinking, 130–131
differentiation
    chatbots for, 40, 105
    of process and product, 92–94
    and resource curation, 24, 29
digital books, 93
digital citizenship, 52–53, 142–143
digital journaling, 20
digital storytelling, 114
discussions, online
    establishing purpose, 77–78
    norms and expectations, 78
    posting in, 109–110
    types of, 76–77
distance learning, 140
Dive into UDL: Immersive Practices to Develop Expert Learners (Grant & Perez), 104
dynamic graphic organizers, 18–19

early childhood education, 130
Easy EdTech Podcast, 8, 19, 26
ebooks, 10
EdSurge Product Index, 139
EdTech tools and resources
    about, 138–140
    assessment tools for teachers, 165
    to boost productivity, 165
    to build portfolios and share resource collections, 164
    communication and social tools, 167
    for exploring the world, 163–164
    generative AI chatbots, 165
    learning and content management tools, 166
    presentation tools for teachers, 166
    for student creators, 164
    supplemental curriculum resources, 166

EdTech vision and mission statement, 136–137

Edutopia (Wysocki), 40

efficiencies habit, 20

email correspondence, 42–43

embedded items, 9

empathy, 56–58, 61

Engaging Students in Reading All Types of Text (Allyn & Burns), 19

entertainment products, 121–122

Epic, 105

equity and access, 141–142

evaluating digital content
    about, 47–48
    accuracy, 49
    authenticity, 50–51
    authority, 48–49
    digital citizenship, 52–53
    essential ideas and extra tips, 146–147
    examining content, 48–51
    process emphasis in student learning artifacts, 51–52

everyday learning, audience for, 122–123

everyday sharing, 111–112

"Everyone's a Curator Now" (Stoppard), 24

exemplars, 94–95

exit slips, 104, 122–123

exploration of the world
    about, 54–55
    for better understanding, 55–59
    EdTech tools for, 163–164
    empathy, 56–58
    essential ideas and extra tips, 147
    social and emotional learning (SEL) and, 58–59
    video conferencing, 61–64
    virtual field trips, 64–65
    VR and AR, 59–61

extension opportunities, 29

Facebook, 11

fact-check, 16

feedback, 51. *See also* peer feedback

files, curating, 26–27, 28*f*

Flip, 91, 102, 110, 111

Flora, 14

formative assessment, 98–103

#FormativeTech: Meaningful, Sustainable, and Scalable Formative Assessment with Technology (Burns), 100

games, curating, 26

GarageBand, 88, 113

Gemini, 15

generative AI, 36–37, 38. *See also* artificial intelligence (AI); chatbots; generative AI

Genially, 90

Google, 15

Google Arts & Culture, 59

Google Classroom, 31–32

Google Docs, 33

Google Meet, 110

Google Sites, 89

Google Slides, 20

Grammarly, 88

graphic organizers, 18–19, 95–96

graphics, curating, 25–26, 28*f*

"How Generative AI Can Augment Human Creativity" (Eapen et al.), 84

How to Differentiate Instruction in Academically Diverse Classrooms (Tomlinson), 24, 92–93

"How to Foster Deep Listening" (Tyson, Hintz, & Hernandez), 110

How to Help Your School Thrive Without Breaking the Bank (Gabriel & Farmer), 136

hyperlinks, 19

images
    chatbots for generating, 40–42
    as content, 10
    curating, 25, 27*f*

Immersive Reader, 11

iMovie, 91

independence, 126–128

independent study, 127–128

infographics, 89

informational products, 122

input, 37

Instagram, 11, 15

instructional model shifts, 140–141

interactive documents, 19
interactive journaling, 58
interactive panoramas, 26

journaling, 20, 58

"Keep It Simple, Schools" (Reich), 140
keyboard shortcuts, 21
Keynote, 90
keyword searches, 11–13, 17f
Khan Academy, 105
Knowledge Constructors, 34
KWL (Know, Want to Know, Learned)
    charts, 100

"Leading for Equity: 5 Steps from
    Awareness to Commitment"
    (Aguada-Hallberg & Santiago),
    141–142
learning and content management
    tools, 166
learning goals, 28
learning management systems, 31–32
Learning to Choose, Choosing to Learn
    (Anderson), 93–94
links, 9–10
listening in digital spaces, 110–111
live video conferencing, 108–109
Loom, 105

Magic Media, 44
Math Learning Center, 105
media literacy, 142–143
media literacy education, 8
Mentimeter, 100
Merge Cube, 60
microblogging, 10
microphone access, 14
Microsoft Sway, 33, 89, 113
Microsoft Teams, 31
mind mapping, 19
mission statement, EdTech, 136–137
modeling, 94–95, 110, 129
The Motivated Student: Unlocking the
    Enthusiasm for Learning (Sullo), 117
multimedia creations, 90–91
multimodal learning, 86. See also
    creating multimodal artifacts of
    learning

National Association for Media
    Literacy Education (NAMLE), 8
navigating online spaces
    about, 7–9
    accessibility, 11
    audio content, 10
    basic computing skills, 21–22
    chatbot queries, 12, 15–16, 17f
    digital journaling, 20
    embedded items, 9
    essential ideas and extra tips, 145
    extend, 14–15
    graphic organizers, 18–19
    guiding student search experiences,
        11–16
    images, 10
    interactive documents, 19
    keyword searches, 11–13, 17f
    links, 9–10
    microblogging, 10
    organizing information, 16–20, 17f
    primary sources, 15
    shortcuts, 21
    support, 13–14
    synthesizing information, 20–21
    text content, 9
    video content, 10–11
Nearpod, 100
The New Teacher's Companion
    (Cunningham), 135–136
norms and expectations, 78

online discussions
    establishing purpose, 77–78
    norms and expectations, 78
    posting in, 109–110
    types of, 76–77
online spaces, 8. See also navigating
    online spaces
open-ended creation tools, 91–92
open-ended tools, 19
organizing and distributing content,
    31–35
organizing information
    about, 16–18
    graphic organizers, 18–19
    journaling, 20
    mind mapping, 19

originality reports, 52
output, 37

Padlet, 112
peer feedback
    audio and video feedback, 75–76
    giving, 72–73
    receiving and acting on, 73–75
    tips for online, 72
persuasion products, 121
PicCollage, 90
plagiarism, 52
planning instruction
    about, 135–136
    artificial intelligence mindset and,
        143–144
    EdTech tools and resources,
        138–140
    EdTech vision and mission
        statement, 136–137
    equity and access, 141–142
    essential ideas and extra tips, 150
    media literacy and digital
        citizenship, 142–143
    preparing for instructional model
        shifts, 140–141
    "tech-able" moments, 137–138
podcasts, student-created, 87
Poll Everywhere, 100
portfolio-building tools, 164
posting in discussion spaces, 109–110
prerecorded video presentations, 109
presentation tools for teachers, 166
Pressto Writing Assistant, 44, 101
primary sources, 15
problem solving, 129
process differentiation, 92–94
process emphasis in student learning
    artifacts, 51–52, 85
product creation, student. *See* creating
    multimodal artifacts of learning
product differentiation, 93
productivity-boosting tools, 165
productivity prompts, 162
prompt engineering, 37, 84
prompts, chatbot, 37, 41–42, 44–45,
    84–85, 160–162
public spaces, sharing in, 113–114

*The Purposeful Classroom: How to
    Structure Lessons with Learning Goals
    in Mind* (Fisher & Frey), 118

QR codes, 12, 32
QuickTime, 113

recommendations, 73
*Redefining Geek: Bias and the Five
    Hidden Habits of Tech-Savvy Teens*
    (Puckett), 20
reflections and empathy, 58
relevance, 123–124
*The Relevant Classroom: 6 Steps to
    Foster Real-World Learning* (Hardie),
    117
remote collaboration, 69–70
representation, 24
resource collection sharing tools, 164
resource curation
    about, 23–24
    chatbots for, 30–31
    content categories, 25–27, 27*f*–28*f*
    content organization and
        distribution, 31–35
    content selection, 28–29
    essential ideas and extra tips, 146
    students as curators, 34–35
    tools for, 31–32
resource gathering prompts, 161–162
review materials, 43
role-based collaboration, 69–70
rubrics, 95

scavenger hunts, 15
Schoology, 31–32
Screencastify, 105
searches, keyword, 11–13, 17*f*
Seesaw, 18, 20, 31, 102–103, 128
self-differentiation, 93–94
shared-screen collaboration, 69–70
sharing, student
    about, 107–108
    as culminating activity, 112–113
    essential ideas and extra tips, 149
    everyday, 111–112
    listening in digital spaces, 110–111
    in public spaces, 113–114

sharing, student—(*continued*)
  speaking in digital spaces, 108–110
  student branding, 114–115
shortcuts, keyboard, 21
simple searches, 12–13
skills, transferable
  about, 125–126
  adaptability, 132
  app developer thinking, 130–131
  computational thinking, 132–134
  essential ideas and extra tips, 149–150
  independence and autonomy,
    126–128
  independent study, 127–128
  problem solving, 129
  troubleshooting, 131
social and emotional learning (SEL),
  58–59
social justice, 119–120
Soundtrap for Education, 88
Southern Poverty Law Center, 120
specificity, 73
static graphic organizers, 18
Storytelling with Purpose (Hernandez),
  114
student choice, 93–94
student creator tools, 164
student engagement, chatbots and, 39
student interest, 24, 29
student products. *See* creating
  multimodal artifacts of learning
students, as content curators, 34–35
synchronous assessment, 104
synchronous collaboration, 70–71
synchronous discussions, 76
synthesizing information, 20–21

*Tasks Before Apps: Designing Rigorous
  Learning in a Tech-Rich Classroom*
  (Burns), 60–61, 92
*Teach Boldly: Using EdTech for Social
  Good* (Williams), 57
Teaching Students to Drive Their Brains
  (Wilson & Conyers), 126
"tech-able" moments, 137–138
tech fluency, early childhood, 130

text, curating, 25, 27*f*
text-based creations, 88–89
text-based discussions, 76–77
text content, 9
think alouds, 13
Think Big with Think Alouds (Ness), 13
TikTok, 8, 11
time-saving uses for chatbots, 42–43,
  83–84
tools and resources, EdTech. *See*
  EdTech tools and resources
transcripts, audio, 87
transferable skills. *See* skills,
  transferable
troubleshooting, 131

understanding, checking for. *See*
  assessment

values, school, 144
video-based discussions, 77
videoconferencing, 61–64, 108–109
video content, 10–11
video curation, 25, 27*f*
video feedback, 75–76
video presentations, 109
Vimeo, 11
virtual field trips, 64–65
virtual reality (VR), 59–61
virtual reality discussion prompts, 61
vision and mission statement, EdTech,
  136–137
visual creations, 89–90
vocabulary support prompts, 161
voice-to-text, 14

Wakelet, 33
*What Teachers Really Need to Know
  About Formative Assessment*
  (Greenstein), 98
Whole Child Initiative (ASCD), 55

YouTube, 8, 11

Zoom, 88

About the Author

 **Dr. Monica Burns** is a curriculum and EdTech consultant, Apple Distinguished Educator, and founder of ClassTechTips.com. As a classroom teacher in New York City, Monica used digital tools to create an engaging, differentiated learning experience to meet the unique needs of her students. Monica started her blog, ClassTechTips.com, in 2012 to help make EdTech easier for fellow educators and launched the *Easy EdTech Podcast* and her membership site, the Easy EdTech Club, to support educators who want to simplify and streamline technology integration.

Since starting ClassTechTips.com, Monica has led workshops and webinars, and provided keynote presentations to teachers, instructional coaches, administrators, and tech enthusiasts at numerous national and international conferences, including SXSW EDU, ISTE, FETC, and EduTECH. Monica is the author of *Tasks Before Apps: Designing Rigorous Learning in a Tech-Rich Classroom* and four ASCD quick reference guides, including *Using AI Chatbots to Enhance Planning and Instruction* and *Classroom Technology Tips*, among other publications. She can be reached at monica@classtechtips.com and on social media at @ClassTechTips.

An ASCD Study Guide for
EdTech Essentials: 12 Strategies for Every Classroom in the Age of AI, 2nd Edition

This ASCD Study Guide is designed to enhance your understanding and application of the information contained in *EdTech Essentials: 12 Strategies for Every Classroom in the Age of AI, 2nd Edition*.

You can use the study guide after you have read the book or as you finish each chapter. The study questions provided are not meant to cover all aspects of the book but, rather, to address specific ideas that might warrant further reflection and prompt you to make connections with your own classroom practice.

Although you can think about many of this guide's questions on your own, we recommend forming a study group with grade-level colleagues who have read (or are reading) *EdTech Essentials* or using this guide as you read and reflect on the book in a professional learning community (PLC). You can also download a PDF version of this study guide at https://classtechtips.com/studyguide (or scan the QR code).

Study Guide

Chapter 1: Navigate Online Spaces Effectively

1. What online spaces do students currently use during the school day?

2. How do students use video to gather information?

3. Where do students struggle when it comes to evaluating information?

Chapter 2: Curate Resources to Support Every Student

1. What types of content are typically shared with students?

2. How do you handpick resources that are "just right" for students?

3. What system do you use to distribute content to students?

Chapter 3: Generate Ideas and Resources with Artificial Intelligence

1. How do you currently use generative AI to support instructional planning?

2. What goals can generative AI help you support (e.g., differentiating instruction)?

3. How have you refined prompts to make sure you receive the desired result?

Chapter 4: Evaluate Digital Content with an AI Mindset

1. How can you tell if a piece of content is authentic and high-quality?

2. In what ways can you incorporate digital citizenship into conversations about AI in the classroom?

3. How do you currently talk about content attribution with colleagues and students?

Chapter 5: Explore the World with Students

1. What role does empathy play in students' use of digital resources?

2. How can you use different technologies to help students explore a space?

3. In what ways do you or can you use technology to spark student curiosity?

Chapter 6: Collaborate Across Digital Spaces

1. What types of collaboration do students currently participate in?

2. What do synchronous and asynchronous collaboration look like in action?

3. How can you use the "value-adds" technology provides to support student feedback?

Chapter 7: Create Multimodal Artifacts of Learning

1. What is the current balance of consumption and creation in your school or classroom?
2. What types of products can students make to share their learning?
3. How can you differentiate student learning products?

Chapter 8: Assess to Check for Understanding and Pivot Instruction

1. What roles does formative assessment currently play in your school or classroom?
2. How can you take a traditional model and incorporate the "value-add" of technology?
3. How can you "give eyes to an exit slip" this school year?

Chapter 9: Share Student Creations in Big and Small Ways

1. In what ways can or do students participate in live videoconferences or prerecorded videos?
2. What could "everyday sharing" look like in your classroom or school?
3. How could student branding conversations enhance the ways students share their work?

Chapter 10: Connect Students to Authentic Audiences

1. Why is it important to start with the end in mind?
2. What role does the author's purpose play in student work creations?
3. In what ways can you ensure that student work feels authentic and relevant to students?

Chapter 11: Transfer Skills Across Digital Spaces

1. What actions do you or can you take to help students build independence in digital spaces?
2. How can you incorporate independent study opportunities into your work with students?
3. Troubleshooting is an important skill to model. What does this look like in your school or classroom?

Chapter 12: Plan for Tech-Rich Learning Experiences

1. What is your EdTech vision and mission?
2. How have you addressed equity and access concerns, and what is your plan for checking in throughout the school year?
3. How will you decide what belongs in your EdTech tool belt?

ClassTechTips
Newsletter

To hear about the latest EdTech tools and platforms from Monica Burns every Monday, sign up for her free newsletter. Go to www.ClassTechTips.com/Newsletter or scan the QR code.

About ASCD Books

ASCD empowers educators to achieve excellence in learning, teaching, and leading so that each child is healthy, safe, engaged, supported, and challenged. Our books and quick reference guides feature a diversity of seasoned educators and new voices from all areas of the education community on both time-honored and timely topics like classroom management, instructional strategies, leadership, equity, and social-emotional learning. Our publications allow educators to chart their own learning journey so that they and their students can grow and flourish.

About ISTE Books

The International Society for Technology in Education (ISTE) is the leading publisher of books focused on technology in education. Our books and jump start guides promote revolutionary ideas and leading-edge practices that empower learning and teaching in a connected world. They cover a range of edtech topics and tie effective teaching and leadership strategies directly to the ISTE Standards, providing clear, practical guidance to help educators meet the Standards.

Related Resources: Educational Technology

At the time of publication, the following resources were available (ASCD stock numbers in parentheses).

Classroom Technology Tips (Quick Reference Guide) by Monica Burns (#QRG120045)

Demonstrating Student Mastery with Digital Badges and Portfolios by David Niguidula (#119026)

Distance Learning Essentials (Quick Reference Guide) by Monica Burns (#QRG120097)

The eCoaching Continuum for Educators: Using Technology to Enrich Professional Development and Improve Student Outcomes by Marcia Rock (#117048)

Engaging Students in Reading All Types of Text (Quick Reference Guide) by Pam Allyn and Monica Burns (#QRG121059)

Five Myths About Classroom Technology: How do we integrate digital tools to truly enhance learning? (ASCD Arias) by Matt Renwick (#SF115069)

Flip Your Classroom: Reach Every Student in Every Class Every Day, Revised Edition by Jonathan Bergmann and Aaron Sams (#323067) (copublished with ISTE)

Flipping the Learning (Quick Reference Guide) by Jonathan Bergmann (#QRG118053)

Increasing Engagement in Online Learning (Quick Reference Guide) by Stephanie Smith Budhai and Laura McLaughlin (#QRG121063)

The Mastery Learning Handbook: A Competency-Based Approach to Student Achievement by Jonathan Bergmann (#122038)

Principles and Practices for Effective Blended Learning (Quick Reference Guide) by Kristina Doubet and Eric M. Carbaugh (#QRG121056)

Summarization in Any Subject: 60 Innovative, Tech-Infused Strategies for Deeper Student Learning, 2nd Edition by Rick Wormeli and Dedra Stafford (#118048)

Tasks Before Apps: Designing Rigorous Learning in a Tech-Rich Classroom by Monica Burns (#118019)

Using AI Chatbots to Enhance Planning and Instruction (Quick Reference Guide) by Monica Burns (#QRG123066)

For up-to-date information about ASCD resources, go to www.ascd.org. You can search the complete archives of *Educational Leadership* at www.ascd.org/el. To contact us, send an email to member@ascd.org or call 1-800-933-2723 or 703-578-9600.